PREAC
PR

MOWBRAY PREACHING SERIES

Series Editor: D. W. Cleverley Ford

Preaching the Risen Christ: D. W. Cleverley Ford
Preaching through the Acts of the Apostles: D. W. Cleverley Ford
Preaching through the Life of Christ: D. W. Cleverley Ford
Preaching through the Prophets: John B. Taylor
Preaching through Saint Paul: Derrick Greeves
More Preaching from the New Testament: D. W. Cleverley Ford
Preaching on Devotional Occasions: D. W. Cleverley Ford
Preaching on Favourite Hymns: Frank Colquhoun
More Preaching on Favourite Hymns: Frank Colquhoun
Preaching on Special Occasions, Volume 3: Edward H. Patey
Preaching on Great Themes: D. W. Cleverley Ford
Preaching on the Holy Spirit: D. W. Cleverley Ford
Preaching on the Lord's Supper: Encounter with Christ: Ian MacLeod
Preaching on Prayer: Monica Ditmas

Preaching through the Christian Year:
- Volume 9: Robert Martineau
- Volume 10: Brian Hebblethwaite
- Volume 11: Peter Lee
- Volume 12: John M. Turner

Preaching at the Parish Communion:
- ASB Epistles – Sundays: Year One: Robin Osborne
- ASB Epistles – Sundays: Year One, Volume 2: Dennis Runcorn
- ASB Epistles – Sundays: Year Two: Dennis Runcorn
- ASB Epistles – Sundays: Year Two, Volume 2: John Vipond
- ASB Gospels – Sundays: Year One: Dennis Runcorn
- ASB Gospels – Sundays: Year One, Volume 2: Eric Devenport
- ASB Gospels – Sundays: Year Two, Volume 2: Peter Morris

PREACHING ON PRAYER

MONICA DITMAS

MOWBRAY

Mowbray
A Cassell imprint
Villiers House, 41/47 Strand,
London WC2N 5JE, England

First published 1990

British Library Cataloguing in Publication Data

Ditmas, Monica, *1924*–
Preaching on prayer.
1. Christian life. Prayer
I. Title
248.32

ISBN 0–264–67216–X

Typeset by Colset Private Limited, Singapore
Printed and bound in Great Britain by
Biddles Ltd, Guildford and King's Lynn

CONTENTS

FOREWORD

When during the course of 1989 I was discussing with Ruth McCurry, the religious publisher of Cassell, the future of the Mowbray series of preaching books, she made the suggestion that since many women ordained to the diaconate in the Church of England, and others as well, regularly preach in churches on Sundays, would it not be a good time to produce a preaching book written by a woman? The upshot was that I undertook to be responsible for this.

Through Ronald Gordon, the Bishop at Lambeth, I was introduced to Mrs Monica Ditmas, whose work as Warden of the Portsmouth Diocesan Retreat House he had come to value when Bishop of that Diocese. This was her last post before retirement though she is still very active as a counsellor and spiritual director, and conducting Quiet Days in various places. She trained for this with a year's counselling course at Exeter University. Before that, for twenty-five years in all, she was a schoolmistress, first at Parkstone Grammar School, then at the Cheltenham Ladies College, and finally for twelve years as Headmistress of Lord Digby's School, Sherborne, the town's grammar school. She has recently been appointed a Lay Canon of Portsmouth Cathedral. Hers has been a full life providing a wide and varied experience of people, their hopes and their fears, their aspirations and their disappointments.

This book is designed to help those who are called to preach and also, hopefully, readers in general who are concerned to be better equipped for the vital exercise of prayer in its various aspects. He/she would be a rare Christian who did not find spiritual refreshment in its pages.

D.W. CLEVERLEY FORD

INTRODUCTION

There are already so many splendid books on prayer that it may seem absurd to be adding to the list. But, curiously enough, it seems that it is a subject that is rarely preached about. In talking to people I find that many have never heard a sermon on prayer; and have never taken part in any discussion of the subject, except perhaps occasionally on a Lent course. This is partly, I know, because of a sensitive awareness of the need to avoid telling people how they should set about something which is essentially a spontaneous and individual experience. Yet I believe there is a hunger among many to hear more, and not all homes have books in them.

So I hope this collection of sermons may be of some use to anyone who wants to respond to the need. It contains reflections on many different aspects of prayer, reduced to manageable lengths. I have tried, too, to focus on the actual emotional and spiritual needs of people in their everyday lives. As with other books in this series, the anecdotes are personal and anyone using the material will, no doubt, replace them with their own—very likely even more pertinent—experiences.

MONICA DITMAS

The lines on p. 54 are quoted by permission from R. S. Thomas, 'The Word', *Laboratories of the Spirit* (Macmillan, 1975).

1
PRAISE AND ADORATION

As long as I have any being, I will sing praises unto my God.

PSALM 146.1 (BCP)

I remember, when I was thirteen years old, being very astonished at my father's funeral, when it was announced that we would sing some of his favourite hymns, to discover that one of them was 'My God, how wonderful thou art'. I am not sure that I have sung it very often since: it is a good old Victorian hymn, certainly not much in fashion. The last verse goes like this:

Father of Jesus, love's reward,
What rapture will it be
Prostrate before thy throne to lie
And gaze and gaze on thee.

I remember that I was shocked and embarrassed. I looked round at the congregation to see how they were taking it. My sensible, practical, shy, undemonstrative father just lying prostrate and gazing! I could not associate this picture with the real man I thought I knew. Actually, I have realized since that my father was probably rather good at adoring. I think he adored my mother, and was humbly grateful, and even surprised, when he found that his love was reciprocated. In the same way, I suspect that praising and adoring God was a central part of his inner life, and that he never lost his incredulous wonder and joy that his prayer was acceptable, and heard.

1. THE IMPORTANCE OF PRAISE

(a) To be able to 'adore' is certainly one of God's greatest gifts to us, and when we are able to do it from hearts at peace we are momentarily given the experience of love in its most selfless, purest form. When we pray in confusion or anxiety we may be glad, yes, eager, to go into the house of the Lord, but we want something specific in return. But when we pray in joy we are content just to be there. It is enough simply to be with God. More than a thousand years ago a Sufi mystic wrote this prayer:

> O my God
> If I worship thee in desire for heaven
> exclude me from heaven,
> If I worship thee for fear of hell
> burn me in hell,
> But if I worship thee for thyself alone
> then withhold not from me thine eternal beauty.

Our prayers of praise are of enormous value because they keep us in touch with what is real. For the beauty, love and truth which we praise *are* what God actually is. It is surprisingly easy for us to pray every day with steady discipline and yet gradually to lose our vision of who it is we are praying to, to take God for granted. Praise reminds us, as no other form of prayer can do, that we are actually seeking to be in touch with the very source of eternal wisdom and love. If we only confess or make petitions, there is a danger that our God will eventually become a sort of super-psychiatrist or social worker. We have to retain our sense of the numinous, of the glory and mystery of God. And because the need to adore and revere is part of our instinctual heritage, if we no longer find a focus for it in God we tend to displace it on to other human beings. Adoration degenerates into adulation, and we begin to 'worship' pop stars or political leaders—even Hitlers. So praising is an essential activity for us. It is a bit like our daily cleaning of contact lenses or glasses, if we wear them; it keeps our vision clear and uncontaminated. Those of us who do have to perform this daily ritual might well give it a symbolic significance by using it as an opportunity for praise!

(b) But it has been suggested that our praise is an essential need of God's too. This is something that theologians often debate. It may seem odd to us that God should actually desire continually to be told how wonderful he is. We do not much care for this trait if we think we spot it in our fellow human beings! I think we can say with certainty that if God does desire our praise, it is for our sakes, because only if we remain in this truthful relationship with him can there be a mutual interchange of love. But there is one other aspect of God's 'need' to be considered. If we do not celebrate his glory, who will? Just as he has no other hands than ours, so he has no other voices. And, of course, praise is not to be confined to mere words. God is to be praised through all our attitudes and actions, through our whole lives. In the Eucharist we pray that we may show forth his glory in the world. The humbling and extraordinary thing is that God should think us capable of doing so. In that intensely beautiful prayer recorded in the fourth gospel, Jesus on the eve of his death prayed for his disciples. 'I pray for those whom thou hast given me . . .; *through them has my glory shone.*' What! Had Christ's glory already shone through these men who were about to desert him, through Peter the impetuous, through James and John who asked to be first in his kingdom, through Thomas? How, after this, can we dodge our clear responsibility? We have a vocation to proclaim his praise.

2. PRAISING IN DISTRESS

But to offer the prayer of praise when we are joyful is one thing: to do so when we are in grief or distress is quite another. Can we hang on to our sense of who God is, of his glory, even in the dark times? Of course, there are countless examples of people who have done so. We think of Paul and Silas in prison at Philippi, having been thoroughly beaten up the day before. At midnight, bruised and bleeding, in the dark, with their feet in the stocks, we are told that they sang praises to God and that the other prisoners listened to them. But most of us fear that we could never reach such heroic heights. And even if we perceive that human beings are often given a special grace at moments of great drama or tragedy, what about the ordinary miseries, irritations, losses and muddles of our daily lives? At these times, when everything seems to be going wrong, we find it exceedingly difficult to keep on praising. But if we persevere in our efforts to do so, often our apparently empty words do influence and calm our thoughts, and restore our sense of perspective. However, in deep and persistent sorrow it is sometimes best to accept our human limitations and stop struggling. God is still present in our suffering, and since he knows our inmost thoughts, he also knows that losing our ability to praise is a very real part of our deprivation. So it is a time when we can learn another lesson—that prayer is not only our own activity. It is also the activity of the Holy Spirit in our hearts. If we continue to cling to God and to pray as we can, then gradually we begin to perceive small flickering lights in our darkness, lights which we know we did not ourselves kindle. Even in misery we recognize them as signals from that full glory which seems at present many light-years away. They are enough to give us the hope and courage to go on.

Viktor Frankl, a Jewish psychiatrist, has described how when he arrived in Auschwitz he had to surrender his clothes, in which he had hidden the precious manuscript of his first book. He was given instead the worn-out rags of a dead inmate. 'Instead of the many pages of my manuscript, I found in a pocket of the newly-acquired coat a single page torn out of a Hebrew prayer book, containing the main Jewish prayer, the Shema Yisrael.' He knew he was being challenged to *live* his thoughts instead of merely putting them on paper, and this small 'light' from God enabled him to survive all the rigours of the camp. How much strength he found actually to praise God in words during those years, we do not know. He was not immune from the squalor and filth, or from the apathy and irritability of the half-starved. But a few days after the liberation—feeling numb, disorientated, and strangely joyless—he walked through the country towards the market town near the camp.

> There was nothing but the wide earth and the sky and the larks' jubilation and the freedom of space. I stopped, looked around, and up to the sky—and then I went down on my knees. How long I knelt there, memory can no longer recall. But I know that on that day, in that hour, my new life started.

So his praise was restored to him. Many of us, in humbler ways, have had similar experiences. Through them we have begun to acquire the certainty that we will never have to experience paradise lost: it is only paradise deferred. A lifelong depressive, Gonville ffrench-Beytagh, has written, 'You begin not to dread depression. You know it will come, for that is your lot: but there is the knowledge that you will find God again afterwards.' So gradually we find ourselves more able to continue to praise, even in darkness. We realize that the mercy of God is truly infinite. And the day may come when we can say with the full inner conviction of the psalmist, 'As long as I have any being, I will sing praises unto my God'.

2
THANKSGIVING

It is very meet, right, and our bounden duty, that we should at all times, and in all places, give thanks unto Thee, O Lord.

(BCP)

A shared memory of all our childhoods will be that question so constantly directed at us, 'What do you say?' We very soon grasped that the compulsory answer was either 'please' or 'thank you', according to circumstances. We also quickly learned that in this matter, good manners were to take precedence over truth. Of course when the present or kindly gesture was just right there was no problem: we could rush to embrace the giver with spontaneous hugs. But in less favourable situations it was not permissible to say 'I've got it already' or 'I would rather have had a rabbit'. The same code tended to govern our relationship with God. We knew that at bedtime 'Thank you God for a lovely day' must be said, as also, after meals, despite the cabbage, 'Thank you for my good dinner amen'. In later life we began to feel the need to temper our more sycophantic utterances with a degree of sincerity! But the basic rule did nevertheless subtly teach us something of great importance. Saying thank you was 'our bounden duty' because it was not simply a matter of the immediate moment: it had something to do with the preservation of relationships.

This was even more clearly shown when it was our turn to give. It did not even occur to us that the recipients of our raffia baskets, paintings, or bunches of dandelions, might be experiencing the same dilemma. We accepted their rapturous exclamations without question. We were right to do so, for these were highly satisfactory exchanges. There was a tacit awareness, on both sides, that what was being given and received was no mere present: it was an exchange of love.

1. THE IMPORTANCE OF THANKSGIVING

(a) The prayer of thanksgiving has the same significance. It is more than a simple expression of gratitude for particular joys or successes. Of course it is right—and, indeed, absolutely natural—that we should give thanks for these. Katharine Mansfield, a young writer who dared to profess atheism long before it was socially acceptable to do so, nevertheless wrote after her first sight of the Alps, 'If only one could make some small grasshoppery sound of praise to someone, of thanks to someone—but to whom?' But in addition to this, our regular offering of the prayer of thanksgiving affirms our desire to remain in a loving relationship with God, and never to take him for granted, just as we can never take for granted those whom we love on earth. You remember the story of the ten lepers who were healed and the one who turned back to Jesus to give thanks. 'And where are the nine?' Jesus asked. They had all taken their healing for granted: but they were healed just the same. So did it matter? What, if anything, did they miss? The answer is, a great deal. The memory of this event for the man who returned will have been of a quite different order from theirs. This Samaritan had somehow preserved, through all the squalor of his suffering, a sense that how we live matters, and he received from Jesus a unique blessing. To brush off the significant moments of life carelessly is a terrible impoverishment. It is the very opposite of holiness of living. But how often in our thoughtless haste we ourselves would have to be numbered among the nine.

It is a fact of experience that the more we give thanks, thus hallowing the ordinary events of our daily lives, the more we learn to delight in it. It becomes less and less a matter of dutiful good manners. Dr Oliver Sacks wrote of the poet W. H. Auden, who became a Christian in his latter years, that 'a genius for gratitude lay at the very centre of his being'. And not long before his death Auden wrote a final poem containing the line 'Let your last thinks all be thanks'.

(b) There is another important aspect of thanksgiving. It preserves us in a relationship not only of love, but also of truth. It helps us to cling to the knowledge that we have nothing that is truly our own, and thus frees us from the anxious possessiveness that is the cause of so much of our insecurity and fear. 'I thank you that I am not as other men are' was the Pharisee's prayer. But he was not really thanking

God at all: his 'prayer' consisted of self-congratulation. How vulnerable he was in his assumption that all he had—status, prestige, ability, dedication, virtue—was somehow his by right. He did not realize that all he had was God's, and that his value, his identity, did not depend on it, that even if it should all be taken away he could manage without it, provided that he could still receive God's mercy and grace. Paradoxically, the more lightly we sit to our possessions the more we are able truly to give thanks for them, because we perceive more clearly that they are simply tokens of that 'inestimable love' which underlies them—the permanent gift that can never be taken away.

2. THANKFULNESS IN SUFFERING

(a) But as human beings we cannot always feel thankful. How are we to give thanks when our lives are torn apart by tragedy or loss, or in times of humiliation and failure? And is there any meaning at all in thanks that are insincere? People who are perpetually grateful can be intensely irritating. There is often a sort of smug righteousness about them, and we would find it almost a relief to hear them complain! The answer is that God never expects us to deny our feelings. Once when I was in a group discussing the prayer of thanksgiving a woman suddenly said how guilty she felt that she could not give thanks for her husband's death! Questioning revealed that a group of zealous Christians had impressed on her that she must do so, because we are commanded to give thanks always for all things. However, when she was asked if there was anything at all in the situation for which she *could* give thanks, she at once replied fervently, 'Oh, yes!' She was grateful that he no longer suffered; that she had somehow been enabled to keep going and manage on her own; for the comfort and support she had received from her friends; and for occasional moments of awareness of God's presence with her in her sorrow. All that she said, and the evidence of her life, in which there was little sign of bitterness, marked her as a person who still lived to a high degree in a relationship of gratitude with God. When she was assured of this, and that God would not be so absurd as to demand of anyone that they should thank him when a loved person died, her relief was plain. She saw that instead of struggling to give thanks for her husband's death, she could give thanks for his life, and at the same time commit her own future life into God's hands. The action of the Holy Spirit begins where we are and with what we *can* do. God does not expect us to make bricks without straw—he went to great lengths to rescue the Hebrew people from having to do that! What is asked of us is that we should give thanks for the small straws we have. Then we find that, mysteriously, many more are given to us. When I met this woman a few months later, she said that she had found a new peace and acceptance—and she was now giving thanks for that!

(b) But we do not find all non-complainers irritating. Many courageous people even retain a sense of humour in hardship. Recently a programme note for a television comedy series contained samples of what was in store for viewers. Among these was a letter beginning 'I am a senior citizen struggling to make ends meet on a small fixed grin!' Sometimes we sense in others the deep serenity that underlies their suffering. Awareness of God's presence has become so much a part of their lives that it remains with them even in times of desolation. In the gospels of both Mark and Matthew it is recorded that at the end of the Last Supper Jesus and his disciples sang the Passover hymn before setting out for the Mount of Olives and Gethsemane. This hymn was the 'Great Hallel', our Psalm 136, and it is likely that, according to custom, Jesus will have recited the verses with the disciples responding 'Hallelujah!'—'Praise the Lord!'—after each verse. It is a psalm of 27 verses beginning 'O give thanks unto the Lord, for he is gracious: and his mercy endures for ever'. It goes on to chronicle God's merciful acts spanning the history of the Jewish race, and to give thanks for each one. Even while he was thus affirming God's mercy, Jesus will have known that within a few hours he must endure an apparently merciless death. Yet he also trusted that he would pass through this death into that everlasting glory he had shared with his Father from the beginning. God's mercy endured for him, and still does for us. So in times of trouble, when it is hard to give thanks, we may find encouragement in this psalm which has for us such a poignant significance. We may begin to realize what it meant for Jesus to give thanks at all times and in all places—the cost and the glory. And as we look back on our own lives, and perceive, with hindsight, how we have been held and led, even in tragedy and failure, we too may gradually find ourselves able to say 'His mercy endures for ever. Thanks be to God.'

3
CONFESSION

Make me a clean heart, O God, and renew a right spirit within me.

PSALM 51.10 (BCP)

A friend of mine relates that when she was a small girl she and her sister were punished for some misdemeanour by being sent to bed and told to stay there until they were sorry. Her sister managed to be sorry quite soon, but she herself stayed upstairs so long that her father decided to investigate. Hearing his footsteps on the stairs, she called out, 'I'm not sorry, and I'll do it again!' But for us, of course, the point of the story is that the sister, who *was* sorry, will also do it again! There are many difficulties about repentance, turning away from sin, and the chief one is that on our own we cannot do it. We can sympathize with St Paul when he wrote, 'The good which I want to do, I fail to do; but what I do is the wrong which is against my will'.

In one way, we can see that repentance is, or ought to be, simplicity itself. All we have to do is to throw ourselves at God's feet in penitence and receive the forgiveness, mercy and peace that have been freely promised to us. That is true. Yet sometimes we can find this particular form of prayer, this aspect of our communion with God, very difficult. For it is not really a single prayer, but a process, and we may get stuck at either end of it. We may not perceive that we are sinning, and so we cannot confess: or, having confessed, we may not be able to allow ourselves to accept forgiveness. Another difficulty may be that this is a prayer-process that demands time. We cannot confess in impatient haste. We have to be willing seriously to reflect in God's presence.

1. ADMISSION

The first stage of the prayer is that we allow ourselves to perceive not just what we have done or not done but what the flaws and muddles and conflicts are in our inner being. This is not a matter of morbid introspection but of desiring to share our lives with God as truthfully as we can. Of course, we are never going to see ourselves with the clarity with which he sees us, nor will we see precisely what others see. C. S. Lewis once wrote that it is possible for us to practise self-examination for hours without discovering any of those elementary facts about ourselves which are obvious to others after a brief acquaintance! Like many others of my generation, I was given at the time of my confirmation, a little manual containing a questionnaire to be used before receiving communion. Have I lost my temper? Have I told a lie? Have I been slothful or greedy? Have I been considerate to others? I am not sure how much good it did me! I can remember feeling very smug if on any particular occasion a good many answers were in the negative. And such a mechanical approach can encourage a sort of do-it-yourself attitude which is the very opposite of humbly sitting with God and allowing his light to penetrate and permeate our responses. It took me a long time to realize that when we find ourselves repeatedly falling short in a particular area we need to ask why. Sometimes concentrating on our supposed sins prevents us from looking deeper, at the fears and hurts from which they arise, and from seeking the inner healing which we need. If I have a food allergy I will go on having symptoms until I discover which food is causing the trouble and eliminate it from my diet. Similarly, certain situations will always trigger my jealousy or my anger until I discover the root cause and offer it to God for cleansing. Nevertheless, my Saturday night quiz did make the point that we cannot pray the prayer of confession without preparing ourselves to do so.

2. CONTRITION

But of course simply observing and admitting certain facts about ourselves is not the whole story. Perhaps you remember the nursery rhyme enquiry as to who killed Cock Robin. 'I', said the sparrow, 'with my bow and arrow. I killed Cock Robin!' We do not detect much penitence there! It is akin to terrorists claiming responsibility for killings, or the one-upmanship which people feel when they have successfully avoided paying taxes or have 'made a bit on the side'. I have heard many Christian folk cheerfully proclaiming that they will 'never forgive' someone who has wronged them. Curiously, it does not always strike us that our own sins are sins! Sins are what the other fellow commits: we excuse ourselves with 'well, I'm sorry, that's me'. To admit what we have done without contrition is obviously not confession in any meaningful sense. But this does not mean that we ought to indulge in paroxysms of remorse. Often that is not so much a sign of sorrow as of fear, or pride: for either reason we cannot bear to be in the wrong. This was brought home to me once when I quite unjustly lost my temper with a very disturbed pupil with whom I had been trying to build a relationship of trust. I felt that I had destroyed the work of years. While I was confiding my dismay to a friend she suddenly said 'I think you are one of the most arrogant people I have ever met'. I was stunned. Was I not admitting how wrong I had been? 'Yes' she said, 'why should you think that among all human beings you are the one who is always going to get things right?' So we need to have the humility to accept ourselves as the sinners we are and always will be. Our sadness, then, is not due to hurt pride but is the result of our longing to be at one with God, to be infused with his love and grace. When we are in love any estrangement is painful. But the love which gives rise to the sorrow of contrition is also the love which gives us the assurance of forgiveness, and saves us from despair.

3. SEEKING AND ACCEPTING FORGIVENESS

So when we have truly confessed we can ask for God's forgiveness with quiet trust. The gospels stress his boundless love and mercy: he will forgive us for ever. Yet there is still one condition. It is clearly stated in the Lord's Prayer and is, indeed, the only clause in that prayer which Jesus singled out for special emphasis. 'Forgive us our sins, as we forgive those who sin against us.' It is stated again in the parable of the steward who was condemned because he cruelly exacted payment of debts owed to him, although he had been let off his own debts. And this same condition is also found, in a somewhat different but equally challenging form, in Matthew's account of the Sermon on the Mount:

> If, when you are bringing your gift to the altar, you suddenly remember that your brother has a grievance against you, leave your gift where it is before the altar. First go and be reconciled with your brother, and then come back and offer your gift.

When we hear this passage read in church, it is noticeable that we all continue to sit happily in our pews. If we were to take Christ at his word, perhaps our churches ought to empty at this point!

Once when I was taking part in a group discussion of forgiveness, I noticed a woman who was listening in an increasingly angry silence. Suddenly she burst forth 'You don't know what you're talking about. It's all a lot of hot air.' It turned out that her young daughter had been raped and murdered a few years before. In such a situation, humanly speaking, forgiveness is scarcely possible. This woman had not forgiven, did not want to forgive, and I suspect did not want to want to forgive. What she wanted above all else was that the perpetrator of this act should be made to suffer as her daughter had done. But her features and indeed her whole body betrayed the agony that she herself was going through. It was herself, not the rapist, whom she was punishing. She told us that she did continue to pray, and that what she prayed for was that she might cope better, that she might be given some peace. But she felt no peace. Alas, experience shows that in fact we cannot have peace whilst we are vengeful and bitter, however fervently we pray for it. Eventually we have to come to the place of the cross, the place where God forgave those who had tortured and murdered his Son. The death of this Son was 'a full, perfect, and sufficient sacrifice for the sins of the whole world'. The sacrifice is sufficient, and so too is the grace given to us to enable us to forgive as we seek to be forgiven, even though there are times of agony when we find this impossible to believe. So, as we pray for forgiveness for ourselves, we need also to remember in our prayers all those who are trapped in bitterness and are unable to forgive. And with them, all who because of past hurts or deprivations feel themselves to be unacceptable, unforgivable, unlovable, somehow not members of the club. Of all forms of human misery, to be cut off from forgiveness is surely the most tragic, and the sufferers stand desperately in need of our encouragement and unsentimental love.

CONCLUSION

So the true prayer of confession—the opening of our hearts to God and the receiving of his mercy and grace—cannot be a 'quick fix', a brief Saturday night quiz followed by a brief Sunday absolution. It has to be a continuous thread woven into the fabric of our lives, the ceaseless prayer 'Make me a clean heart, O God'. If we begin habitually to live in this open way, we also begin to perceive that we are on a journey. It is a journey towards self-knowledge, which is also a journey towards God, in which our jealousies and angers and prejudices can be gradually offered up and burned away. And all the time we know that although it is we who are travelling, the impetus for the journey is not coming from us. It is God who is drawing us closer to himself. Let us indeed give thanks that in Christ we have been given 'the means of grace and the hope of glory'. Our lives are in safe hands.

4
PETITION

If you dwell in me, and my words dwell in you, ask what you will, and you shall have it.

JOHN 15.7 (NEB)

If you ask people what mode of prayer comes most readily and naturally to them, there are a surprising number who answer 'praise and thanksgiving'. That is a remarkable and encouraging fact. But the majority say—sometimes a little shamefacedly—that the most natural form of prayer for them is to ask God for something. Of course it *is* natural for us to pray for a safe journey or for success in our job interview or for the well-being of someone we love. Yet it is a form of prayer which is also, in a sense 'difficult', because it gives rise to some profound questions, and there is not always much agreement about the answers. Of course we do not need to be continually analysing our prayer: that is like pulling up plants to see if they are growing well. But if we are never willing to examine what we are doing, how can we obey the commandment to love God with our hearts and with our minds, too?

1. MAKING REQUESTS

(a) So let us look for a moment at some of the different attitudes people have to petitionary prayer. When I was working as warden of a retreat house, a place of prayer to which many guests came, I had the opportunity to learn about many of these at first hand. I remember in particular one group who talked about 'winning prayers'. By this they meant prayers which persuaded God to give them what they asked for. They took their stand firmly on the words of Jesus recorded by St Matthew, 'Ask, and it shall be given you'. In this instance they were asking that one of their members, who was about to join a mission to the Jews, might have success in converting them. I am sure they did not think that God was unaware of the situation, nor that he lacked the ability to carry out his intentions unaided. Nevertheless, there was a strong feeling that in some way the outcome depended on the quality of their prayer. If they had enough faith and persistence they would persuade God to act in the way they desired, and to act instantly, here and now.

There was much about this group to rejoice God's heart. First, their zeal and commitment. They truly had that 'hearty desire to pray' of which Cranmer wrote. And they showed faith and persistence of a kind for which there is much biblical support: in fact they would have said they had been commanded by God through his Word to pray in the way they did. It is clear that many Old Testament writers believed God did change his mind in response to human urgings, even repenting of his previous behaviour. The gospels, too, show Jesus as sometimes modifying his initial response under pressure, for instance in the case of the Syro-Phoenician woman whose clever repartee so impressed him. Above all Jesus stressed the importance of faith: it could achieve the apparently impossible, even moving mountains. And as to persistence, you will remember the story of the householder who reluctantly got out of bed and gave his neighbour a loaf, because he could not stand the continuous knocking. There are many more instances we could give. Yet after affirming all this, I was still left with some questions about the nature of this 'winning prayer'.

My misgivings arose from the fact that it never seemed to cross anyone's mind that their diagnosis of a problem, or their proposed solution to it, might possibly be wrong. They assumed without question that God saw things the way they did. What was missing was humility—that complete surrender to God which pervaded all that Jesus said or did. His prayer was always that God's will might be done. In the same way the *Book of Common Prayer* qualifies the request that God will fulfil the desires of his servants with the rider 'as may be most expedient for them'. So here we see faith of a different kind: the faith that God knows best.

(b) How detailed, then, ought our requests to be? In the Lord's Prayer we are taught to ask simply and briefly for our essential needs: just bread and forgiveness! There are obvious difficulties about being too specific. One is that if we ask God to intervene and arrange events to suit us, someone else may have to be deprived or hurt. If I get a glorious day for my daughter's wedding, in what I take to be a direct answer to my prayer, then what about my neighbour who has been praying for rain to perfect his blooms for the flower show? A rather ribald verse written during the First World War sums up the dilemma:

> God heard the embattled nations sing and shout
> 'Gott strafe England' and 'God save the King!'
> God this, God that, and God the other thing.
> 'Good God' said God, 'I've got my work cut out!'

It is easy to cheapen our prayer until the bestowal of God's grace begins to seem like a lottery in which we might be lucky enough to draw the winning ticket. The process savours more of 'magic' than of love and mercy. Perhaps the best safeguard we can have in all this is to learn to laugh at ourselves! You may know the story of the little girl who was found kneeling by her bed reciting the alphabet. She explained that she did not know what to say, so she was giving the letters to God for him to arrange. God can make sense of our nonsense, sifting our most naïve petitions for the grains of devotion they contain. We need not fear that he will be deflected from his steady course by our absurdities.

2. OBSERVING GOD AT WORK

But petition may be misused in other ways which receive less attention but have more serious consequences. One danger arises if we are focusing too narrowly on our own solution to a problem. As human beings we have a tendency to see what we want or expect to see and very little else. Se we may fail to observe what God is actually doing in response to our prayer, and thus fail to take appropriate action ourselves. There is a passage in the autobiography of the Russian author Konstantin Paustovsky which movingly illustrates this. He is describing peasant women praying at a midnight mass in Lublin at Easter, 1915:

The only expression we could see in their eyes was their fervent

> expectation of a miracle, their enormous hope that perhaps this child, or this pale woman with sad eyelashes who was the mother of the infant God, would banish war, exhausting work and poverty from the world. . . . Despite common sense, despite their experience of life, they passionately believed that justice had become incarnate in the person of the poor wanderer from Galilee, in the person of God. They needed this God in order to make sense of the murderous muddle of human existence, but for some reason he delayed to speak, to act. He stood aside from their lives. They believed in him nevertheless, though his inaction had lasted for centuries.

We cannot doubt God's love for these women, nor their devotion. So what had gone wrong? Why was their prayer not answered? Were they waiting in vain? Perhaps we have to change the question, and ask, instead, 'Why were they waiting at all?' For the problem often lies, not in the inactivity of God, but in his activity not being noticed, and thus not being used to spur and direct our efforts. Perhaps God was waiting for *them*. There may have been a potential Florence Nightingale or Elizabeth Fry among them. The message of the incarnation and of the gift of the Holy Spirit is that God is with us *now*. He may reveal himself in a growing movement towards social justice, but also in an infinite number of other ways. Bishop John V. Taylor has said that mission consists of 'discovering what God is doing in the world and doing it with him'. We need to incorporate something of this attitude into our petitionary prayer.

3. LETTING GOD TAKE CHARGE

A second danger, paradoxically, is most likely to arise for people who have started off with great faith in the power of prayer. Without realizing it, they may come to regard prayer as a do-it-yourself activity in which they themselves are responsible for obtaining the 'correct' answers. This can create much anxiety, especially when it is healing for which they have prayed. They may recall the many occasions when Jesus said 'Your faith has made you whole'. But faith comes in many forms, and so does healing. To suppose that we have to *earn* an answer to prayer is to turn the gospel message on its head. If Jesus can be said to have had an especially soft spot for anyone, it was for those very people who thought themselves failures and of no account. Praying in faith does not have to mean praying in the conviction that our prayer will be granted in the form we have asked. Above all it means praying in the faith that we are being *heard*, and heard with love. What is to come after that is not in our hands.

So prayer may have zeal, faith, persistence, all those splendid qualities. But to these must be added the most vital ingredient of all, our own surrender to God. Only when we are completely 'in Christ', perfectly attuned to his will, can we expect our views and his always to coincide. Meanwhile, if we persevere, it often happens that we find our petitions becoming simpler. We ask with more and more fervour for less and less, until at last the single petition 'Be with me, Lord' seems to cover everything else and is all we need to say. 'If you dwell in me, and my words dwell in you, ask what you will, and you shall have it.' Lord, if I may indeed dwell in you, and your words in my heart, I think I shall not have much need of my own words any more, nor anything further to ask. Even so, come, Lord Jesus.

5

INTERCESSION

It is not for these alone that I pray, but for those also who through their words put their faith in me.

JOHN 17.20 (NEB)

In three of the closing chapters of the fourth gospel we are given the farewell message of Jesus to the Twelve, and then the prayer in which he committed them to his Father's care. 'They are still in the world, and I am on my way to thee. Holy Father, protect by the power of thy name those whom thou hast given me. . . .' His love for them shines out clearly, not only divine love but human love too. He describes them as God's gift to him during his life on earth. But Jesus did not end his intercession there. 'It is not for these alone that I pray.' Just as light from a star may reach us from space thousands of years later, so across a span of centuries we can hear the voice of Jesus praying for *us*. Surely we do not need to be persuaded further of the value of intercession. It comes to us as the authentic voice of love.

It has been understood in this way by countless numbers of men and women ever since. Many of us could relate from our own experience how much it has meant to us in times of anxiety or distress to know that someone is praying for us. Even though physically we may be completely cut off, some inner telepathy gives us this certainty. When we keep vigil and light candles for captives and hostages whose whereabouts are unknown, who are isolated from the world, we cherish the hope that they will know we are holding them before God, and that this will give them courage to struggle on. Gonville ffrench-Beytagh has written of his time in prison in South Africa:

> Underlying my panics and weeping-fits and fear, there was a sense of immense strength upholding me, and surrounding me like a wall. Later, of course, I found that Christians all over the world, including many religious communities, had been praying for me. I did not know this at the time, but I did feel quite certainly that I was surrounded by a wall of prayer.

So praying for people is a powerful way of expressing our love and concern for them. Is it anything more? Can our intercession not only give support to others, but actually take away their pain, alter their circumstances, cause them to change their ways if they are in sin or error, even save their lives? On this point there is controversy among Christians. But it is impossible to read the New Testament without feeling that the answer given there is unhesitatingly 'yes'.

You will remember the occasion when Jesus came down from the Mount of Transfiguration to find the disciples surrounded by a hostile crowd. They had failed to cure an epileptic boy. Later when they asked Jesus what had gone wrong, he told them that they had not prayed enough. Clearly the disciples took this lesson to heart. All the evidence is that after Our Lord's death they had complete faith in the power of intercessory prayer. James, the brother of Jesus, who became one of the leaders of the infant Church, wrote an open letter to Jewish converts giving them, among much else, some explicit instruction in prayer.

> Is one of you ill? He should send for the elders of the congregation to pray over him and anoint him with oil in the name of the Lord. The prayer offered in faith will save the sick man, the Lord will raise him from his bed, and any sins he may have committed will be forgiven. A good man's prayer is powerful and effective.

That is the basis for the revival of the ministry of healing which is taking place in many churches today. And in all our corporate worship we regularly offer intercessions, having in mind the words of Jesus recorded by Matthew:

> I tell you this: if two of you agree on earth about any request you have to make, that request will be granted by my heavenly Father. For where two or three have met together in my name, I am there among them.

We know that, as in the earliest days, whenever Christians meet they still have stories to exchange of the ways in which their prayers have been wonderfully fulfilled.

Yet it is not always so. Even in the New Testament there are examples of prayer apparently not being answered. St Paul tells us that he three times begged the Lord to heal him of some sharp bodily pain, but it was not granted. There are many people, including many Christians, who have felt at some time in their lives that there was no blessing for them. If we say that we will pray for people in severe distress they may even be angry, regarding it as a patronizing response. What good will it do? They have prayed and prayed and nothing has changed. Even St Teresa, a staunch disciple, had to say to God on one occasion, 'Lord, if this is how you treat your friends, it is no wonder that you have so few of them!' Why is there famine in Africa, where thousands of black Christians pray for their daily bread? Why is there drought? Elijah may have been successful when he prayed for rain, but in our parish church we have prayed for the ending of drought for years, and still people die. When we pray for others, as when we pray for ourselves, we can often feel that we are praying in vain. So is God randomly inconsistent? Of course not. We have to look for an explanation of this paradox at a far deeper level, and to look not only at God but at ourselves.

2. ANSWERS TO PRAYER

One reason for our pleas for others apparently not being met is that we may be hopelessly 'off-target' in discerning what they need. I once visited an old lady in hospital who confided to me her distress that people in her church were praying for her recovery. 'They don't understand', she said, with tears, 'that I'm ready for the Lord to take me now.' She was genuinely afraid that their prayers would keep her alive! But God in his mercy knew better, and she died peacefully in her sleep that night. It is important that we do not assume that we know what is for the best. Often it is wiser simply to hold people before God, knowing that he will understand their deep needs far better than we do.

But we do not have to worry, as that old lady did, that God will be swayed by our misguided prayers. He is well able to extract from them what is good and usable and discard the rest. St Augustine in his *Confessions* gives a good example of this. His mother, Monica, regarded prayer for her son's salvation as virtually her life's work. All through his wayward youth she kept on interceding for him. On one occasion she was deeply distressed that he was proposing to go to Rome—and without her! Neither of them had any idea at this time that this was to be a turning point in his life, a severance from all that in the past had held him back. Augustine simply wanted to go. And the only way he could do this was to slip away secretly one night, leaving his mother—who I think was a rather possessive lady as well as a saint!—weeping and praying. She begged God to prevent him sailing. But, says St Augustine, God ignored this petition in order that he might give her what had always been her chief desire. Monica felt at the time that God had failed her; but years afterwards she understood how greatly, in this apparent deprivation, she had been blessed.

We know, too, what the sequel was to God's rejection of St Paul's request for physical healing. Paul came to understand that he had received the most loving answer of all. It was 'My grace is all you need: power comes to its full strength in weakness'. So Paul was freed from fear, for life. Thereafter he knew that nothing could separate him from God's love, and that outward circumstances could never take from him the grace that was within his heart.

We can be sure that God will never give us a stone when we ask for bread: but it is often hard for us to recognize the bread. Manna from heaven may at first seem to be strange and alien food. Paul Theroux tells a story about a traveller in South America who arrogantly proclaimed that *he* did not see any snakes. 'Maybe not', an old man replied, 'but they saw you!' The fact that we do not see God in events does not mean he is not there!

3. SELF-OFFERING

So the faith that underlies our intercessions is not simply faith that there will be a miracle, but faith that God is in charge. He may not intend a change in our circumstances, but in ourselves. Jesus took infinite care that people should not focus too much on the miraculous elements in his ministry. How often he said to someone he had healed, 'Keep this to yourself'. He did not want the wrong sort of publicity which would mislead people about the nature of God and of his kingdom. God must be honoured above all for his goodness. We, too, must be very sure, when we intercede, that we do not offer a desperate world 'magic' instead of love.

For if we take it seriously, intercession is costly for us, too. We cannot use it as a means of avoiding having to do anything ourselves. Neville Ward wrote: 'To ask in Christ's name that God's will be done in the world involves at the same time offering ourselves to God, to be truly part of that through which he intends to answer prayer for the world's salvation'. And here is Evelyn Underhill, even more formidably succinct: 'The prayer that is mere request without self-offering is not prayer "in Christ's name" and is not worth the time it takes to say'.

When we intercede we are putting ourselves at risk. We are placing ourselves at God's disposal, and we cannot tell in advance what will be asked of us. As St Paul wrote to the Galatians, 'God is not to be fooled'. It is no use praying for world peace if we are at the same time tolerating gossip, back-biting and petty quarrels in our own communities. When we pray 'Lord, make us instruments of thy peace', it is not enough that we are moved by the beauty of the words, and then go away and leave the follow-up to God. Jesus prayed for his disciples, and for us: but he also gave his life. Give us grace, in this as in all else, to follow your example, Lord.

6
MEDITATION

Thy words have I hid within my heart.
PSALM 119 (BCP)

When Jesus was asked by a scribe which commandment was the first of all, his answer was to recite the great Jewish prayer, the *Shema Yisrael*, taken from the fifth book of the Law, known to us as Deuteronomy. 'Hear, O Israel: the Lord our God, the Lord is one: and you shall love the Lord your God with all your heart, and with all your soul, and with all your mind, and with all your strength.' The Jews were commanded in the Law to have these words 'upon their hearts', and to bind them to their hands and foreheads and write them on the doorposts of their houses and on the gates. It is no wonder that they attached such importance to them. It is hard to imagine a more beautiful description of the ways in which we are to respond to God.

But there is one phrase whose meaning is not entirely obvious. How are we to love God 'with all our minds'? One answer would be that we are to study the scriptures and to think and reflect about the nature of God and of faith with as much integrity as we can and with a thirst for truth. Undoubtedly that is a part of it. But it is possible to be a brilliant theologian or Bible scholar, to know or surmise a great deal about God, even to think about him constantly, without ever truly loving him. He is simply an object of speculation or religious curiosity. The purpose of the prayer of meditation is to transform all our thinking into an exercise in love. Through it we offer all the differing faculties of minds—our perception, reason, memory, imagination, and even our awareness of physical sensation—for God to illuminate and bless, and to use in any way he desires.

1. THE IMPORTANCE OF MEDITATION

Yet many of us go through our lives without ever praying in this way or perhaps even knowing what the term 'meditation' means. If we think of it at all, we probably connect it with the East, with Yoga, or with a visual image of a remote Buddha-figure sitting in the lotus position in stony silence. It is a form of prayer that has been so much neglected in the West in recent centuries that it comes as a surprise to many people to discover that a Christian tradition of meditation even exists. We may dimly recall the names of some of the great teachers of the past—St John of the Cross, Ignatius Loyola—but we no longer have any idea what they taught. Perhaps we would not be far off the mark if we attributed the bitterness, prejudice, and failure to discern priorities, evidenced in so much recent ecclesiastical controversy, to this neglect. We are using our minds, perhaps even over-using them, but we are not loving God with them. Despite their devotion to the commandment, the Jews did not always get this right either. Jesus severely criticized the Pharisees for their loveless use of the Law, and was wryly amused at the scholarly Nicodemus, who was so dependent on logic and reason that an appeal to his imagination left him completely baffled. Surrendering our minds to God does not mean that we are expected to deny our insights or fudge what, at any particular stage of our pilgrimage, we believe to be the truth. It does mean that we are to be reflective, attentive, self-critical people, quietly sorting out our thoughts, intuitions and life-experiences in God's presence. However great our devotion to the scriptures, if we do not pray and meditate in this way we are in danger of using them for our own purposes, rather than letting them use us.

2. WHAT MEDITATION INVOLVES

(a) The fact that meditation is not widely used often leads people to assume that it is 'difficult', beyond the capacity of ordinary mortals, and suitable only for a small élite. Sadly, its practitioners sometimes appear to share that view! Certainly it comes more naturally to some people than to others, but there is no intrinsic difficulty about it. It can be used by anyone who has sufficient desire. The only difficulty lies precisely there: to have sufficient desire. For although not difficult it *is* demanding. Unlike prayers of thanksgiving or petition which can be offered as swift 'arrow' prayers, meditation requires time, quiet, and concentration, and, in the early stages at least, some guidance, either from books, or, preferably, from someone who already has experience of it. Cranmer wrote that we should 'read, mark, learn, and inwardly digest', and digestion cannot be hurried. Ten minutes is the absolute minimum: thirty is better, and an hour better still. And although it is possible to meditate in a crowded, noisy place, most of us need to find a quiet spot where we can be free from interruption—a hillside, as Jesus did, or a bedroom, or even a church, if there is one we can visit on our way to the shops or in the office lunch hour. But if we truly want to learn to meditate, the only thing to do is somehow to begin, despite the practical difficulties. If we wait until we are 'ready', or until it is convenient, we may wait for ever. The poet Rabindranath Tagore wrote:

> The song that I came to sing remains unsung to this day.
> I have spent my days in stringing and unstringing my instrument.

We can all recognize ourselves here!

(b) Having found the time and place, we need to 'center down', as Americans would say, and find a relaxed position, so that we will not be interrupted by the discomfort of our bodies. Often they will become calm more easily if we concentrate for a while on the quiet rhythm of our breathing. Then we can take a passage of scripture, or a psalm, hymn, poem or prayer, or even a single word or phrase, and repeat it slowly to ourselves with close attention. The object is not to see how much ground we can cover, but how deep we can go: Dietrich Bonhoeffer recommended spending a whole week on a single text. Then we can start our meditation by using our intellect, focusing on the meaning of the passage and, if necessary, looking up any difficult words or allusions in any reference book we may have. The next step is to allow our memory and imagination to bring into our minds other linked events or experiences or associations. Suppose we have chosen a verse from Psalm 18, 'Thou also shalt light my candle: the Lord my God shall make my darkness to be light'. We might actually light a candle, and as we watch its flame receive a clear childhood memory of singing 'Jesus bids me shine with a clear, pure light'. Or we might think of the fourth gospel, 'The light shines in the darkness, and the darkness has not overcome it': or of Bishop George Appleton's prayer, 'Give me a candle of the spirit, O God, as I go down into the deep of my own being'. In this way, by unhurriedly using all the powers of our mind, we allow the passage to disclose to us its full, deep meaning, and we reflect on what it is telling us about God, and about our own nature and our own lives. Can I accept with joy that God will light my candle? What darkness in my life, now, do I want Christ to dispel?

Finally, we make an offering of all our thoughts—and this is where meditation becomes prayer—and ask that they may be a means of grace for us, to give us clearer insights and draw us closer to God. We need, then, to wait quietly in his presence, not struggling after any particular result, but simply placing ourselves in his hands. Sometimes we may know at once that something of importance has been shown to us—not necessarily something joyful: often it is something we do not much want to see, but we recognize it as truth. More often there is a feeling that we have been fed and nourished, although we cannot say precisely how. But as with all our prayer, we are not responsible for the outcome. It is rare for us to be fully conscious of the activity of the Holy Spirit within us. But the experience of those who regularly pray in this way is that they grow in understanding of themselves and others, become less anxious and erratic in their behaviour, more trusting, a little wiser, in fact. They know that there is a change, and that Christ is becoming the sure foundation for their lives.

(c) Of course, this is only the briefest of indications as to what meditation means. It has many other forms, some of them, like those recommended in the *Spiritual Exercises* of Ignatius Loyola, involving an even greater use of imagination and fantasy. But meditating is never just enjoying 'holy' feelings. It is always a path to truth. The point is well made in John Betjeman's autobiographical poem, 'Before the Anaesthetic', in which facing the possibility of death suddenly reveals to him the superficiality of what he had thought to be true meditative prayer, but which had only been aesthetic self-indulgence:

> Illuminated missals—spires—
> Wide screens and decorated quires—
> All these I loved, and on my knees

I thanked myself for knowing these
And watched the morning sunlight pass
Through richly stained Victorian glass
And in the colour-shafted air
I, kneeling, thought the Lord was there.
Now, lying in the gathering mist
I know that Lord did not exist;
Now, lest this 'I' should cease to be,
Come, real Lord, come quick to me.

We may indeed use 'richly stained Victorian glass' as a focus of attention to still us and direct our thoughts. But we must never forget the vital second step. The gospel stories show Mary, the mother of our Lord, as someone who habitually looked beneath and beyond the immediate event with a deep longing to understand, born out of her love for her son. She loved him with all her mind. In the prayer of meditation we express this same longing. And if we persevere we may find ourselves able truthfully to say, with Mary and with the psalmist, 'Thy words have I hid within my heart'.

7

CONTEMPLATION AND THE PRAYER OF SILENCE

Speak, Lord, for thy servant hears.
1 SAMUEL 3.9 (RSV)

I have a habit of writing in the margins of books—of my books, I hasten to add. I usually manage not to write in other people's! The other day I came across a book I had not opened for many years. It was by a contemplative, telling of the peace and joy, yet also self-exposure and even pain, that could be experienced as a result of encountering God in this form of silent, listening prayer. I found that I had written underneath, 'How much am I willing to pay?'

Why was I afraid, and what was the cost that I envisaged? Partly, perhaps, I feared that I might have to 'pay' with boredom or embarrassment, or that I would find silence very difficult. I have since discovered that this is a reaction many people share. But, beyond this, I had a faint awareness that it would prove impossible to be silent with God unless I had a sincere longing to be totally surrendered to him. In human relationships we can usually manage to *talk* even to little-known acquaintances, but being comfortably silent with people is a different matter. This only happens when we are completely at ease, and it is only with someone we deeply love that we can share the full beauty of silent communion. So it is in our relationship with God.

1. VENTURING INTO SILENCE

(a) But I had no need to be afraid. We never have anything to fear at God's hands, and especially not in prayer. 'O make but trial of his love', says the hymn. If we have the least inclination to be with God in the prayer of silence, and if we dare to attempt it, we shall find that our anxieties are soon dispelled. 'Well do I know', wrote Julian of

Norwich, 'that the more that the soul sees God, the more by his grace does it want him.' In the presence of love we are not condemned, but affirmed and healed.

So is this way of praying for everyone? Certainly temperament plays its part. Silence will always come more naturally to some than to others, and this should never be made a cause of guilt. Within our individual lives, too, our need or desire for silence varies in intensity. But for some there comes a time when words—even words that have meant a great deal to them in the past—seem to be a heavy burden, a barrier, almost, between themselves and God. Often they are dismayed: their prayer seems to be drying up. Of course, there may be other reasons for this—weariness or stress or guilt. But if reflection reveals no such cause, then allowing ourselves to enter into silence is like a liberation. Suddenly our spirits are free. As Mother Julian writes,

> Then we care no longer about praying for anything; for the whole reason why we pray is summed up in the sight and vision of him to whom we pray. Wondering, enjoying, worshipping, fearing—and all with such sweetness and delight that during that time we can only pray in such ways as he leads us.

But not everyone is called to silence in this unmistakable way. If we feel ourselves in any way drawn to it, then we should simply begin. There is now a huge body of literature on the subject, telling us how we can more easily become quiet and still, and empty ourselves of our own preoccupations. Such advice can be of great assistance to us. But experience remains our best teacher—which, of course, is another way of saying that God himself will show us the way.

(b) Above all, we should not think of silence as something we have to struggle to achieve. Struggle increases the very tensions from which we are trying to escape. We are not asked to go out and search for God, like sheep roaming the hillside looking for the lost shepherd. His spirit is already within us. So silence is something we already possess: we have simply to allow ourselves to tune in to it. The Indian poet Rabindranath Tagore struck just the right note when he wrote:

> I ask for a moment's indulgence to sit by thy side. The works that I have in hand I will finish afterwards. . . . Now it is time to sit

> quiet, face to face with thee, and to sing dedication of life in this silent and overflowing leisure.

and again

> I shall wait in the dark, spreading my mat on the floor, and whenever it is thy pleasure, my Lord, come silently and take thy seat here.

So there is no hurry, no sense of deadline or of a task to be accomplished. We slide into a deep listening silence in the same effortless way that we slide into sleep. We are entering into the presence of love.

2. LOOKING AT GOD

You will know the story of the old man who was asked what he did as he sat for a long time unmoving in a church pew. 'Oh', he said, 'I just looks at Him and He just looks at me.' Often people have thought of this contemplative prayer as 'looking at God'. It is a bit like the sort of looking that field naturalists do, a loving, attentive contemplation devoid of any wish to manipulate or change or possess. In a poignant passage in his novel *The Power and the Glory*, Graham Greene describes how the whisky priest learned to love his fellow human beings:

> When you visualised a man or woman carefully you could always begin to feel pity—that was a quality which God's image carried with it. When you saw the lines at the corner of the mouth, how the hair grew, it was impossible to hate. Hate was just a failure of the imagination.

The young French philosopher, Simone Weil, suggested that such complete, selfless, absorbed attention to things and people as they are is the highest form of love. In the silence this is the kind of love which, through his grace, we are enabled to offer to God. We are not, for the moment, making any demands on him. It is enough that he is there, and we are in his presence.

3. LISTENING TO GOD

So when people ask 'But what is the silence *for*?', we can only reply that it has no specifically identifiable purpose, like, say, intercession, or giving thanks. It is simply a way of being with God. But such prayer does have identifiable results. One is that we are enabled to listen, in a way that is not possible when we are talking all the time. Yet if we are honest we may have to admit that we find the idea of 'listening' puzzling, too. Just what are we supposed to hear? Are we to expect an actual voice, speaking aloud to us as another human being would do? The story of the child Samuel suggests exactly this, since three times he thought he was being called by Eli the priest. Many of us will have known something similar, when a thought strikes us with such forceful impact that it is almost as if it had been spoken aloud, and afterwards we cannot be sure whether or not it was so. It is easy to understand why people often declare—and often too glibly and readily—that they have 'a word from the Lord'. In such cases there must always be further careful prayer and testing. Samuel's message, or intuition, was that he must say to Eli some painful and difficult things. In such a case we might unknowingly be prompted by our own subconscious malice, or envy, rather than by God. So when thoughts appear unbidden in our minds a degree of scepticism is necessary at first. Such messages are always in part from God, in that they draw our attention to something we need to reflect about. But they may not always be his final and complete message, the message of pure love. That we can only discover with certainty by remaining quietly and patiently in his presence until it is confirmed to us that our intuitions are arising solely from his love and truth.

But more often God speaks to us in the silence, not with such direct commands, but almost imperceptibly. We may not feel we have 'heard' anything at all, yet afterwards we find that our attitude to those around us, or to our immediate problems and tasks, is subtly different. Somehow we have become more attuned to his will. We have more certainty, more peace. And as the days, weeks and years go by, we may begin to realize that our inner selves have been deeply and permanently changed, we do not know precisely how. 'How silently, how silently, the wondrous gift is given!' The fact that we do not know is in itself a tremendous reassurance. It is not something we have done ourselves. It is as if by simply being with God we have absorbed something of his love.

4. AN ACTIVITY OF LOVE

And our silence can embrace more than ourselves. 'It is in deep solitude that I find the gentleness with which I can truly love my brothers', wrote the monk Thomas Merton. Often we can bring others with us into the silence, with their needs and griefs, not using speech, but simply holding them steadily before God.

The story does not even end there. Because of its emphasis on passivity and surrender, people often fear that to pray in this contemplative way will make us into mere observers of life, choosing to opt out from its painful struggles. But experience shows that the opposite is the case. We become activated in body, mind and spirit. Quakers stress the need to enter into the listening silence more than any other group, and the impact they have had in social reform has been out of all proportion to their numbers. Having heard God speak, Samuel had to act. When we say 'Speak, Lord, for thy servant hears' we are making a total commitment. In contemplation and the prayer of silence it is not just our minds and hearts, but our whole lives, that we are offering to God.

8
PRAYING IN TONGUES

O Lord, open our lips: and our mouths shall proclaim your praise.

(ASB)

The idea that praying is a human activity, something we ourselves do, goes very deep in us. Most of us have been taught in childhood to 'say *our* prayers', and that is what we have continued to do ever since. However, we recognize that there is also a passive element. When we pray we desire to surrender ourselves to the working of the Holy Spirit within us. And there are two forms of prayer, in particular, which arise from this surrender: the prayer of silence and praying in tongues. Although superficially they are so unalike, they have a good deal in common. They represent, in their different ways, what may happen when we acknowledge that we have run out of our own resources entirely, and have no adequate words or even thoughts of our own with which to praise God, or express our love for him, or our deep consciousness of his love for us, or our longing that he will reach out to others.

Once at a church gathering I heard a young woman quietly describe how the gift of tongues had come to her, quite unexpectedly. She had been singing with others in a group on an especially joyful occasion, and suddenly found herself praising with strange sounds and phrases not of her own conscious making. With this came a sense of freedom and release and great joy. She felt that she was indeed praising God at a deep level she had not experienced before. At the same time it all felt very normal and natural. She was not in any sort of trance but was perfectly composed and alert. When she realized later that other Christians regarded this way of praying—and indeed, now, regarded her—with wariness and suspicion, she was puzzled and sad. Was it not a mode of prayer that was specifically endorsed and even encouraged in the New Testament? However, she soon realized that in order to be sure that she was using her gift lovingly and responsibly, without causing offence to others, she would have to keep very quiet about it and pray in this way only when alone. So for years—and this was very painful for her—it had to remain a secret gift, until a small nucleus of charismatic Christians formed in her neighbourhood, among them several people who habitually prayed or sang in tongues, and she was able to join in fully for the first time.

1. WHAT IT MEANS

(a) What, then, is happening when we pray in tongues? It is important, first, to be clear that the young woman was quite right in supposing that in the early church it was very common, if not universal, and was regarded as one of the most important signs of the activity of the Holy Spirit in a Christian community. For instance, while Peter was in the house of the Roman centurion, Cornelius—an extraordinary event in itself—we are told that his audience, while he was still talking to them, 'began to speak in tongues of ecstasy and acclaim the glory of God'. This was one of the incidents Peter subsequently used to convince the Council of Jerusalem that God was calling Gentiles as well as Jews into the church. Later, Paul had a very similar experience in Ephesus, where twelve converts spoke in tongues when he laid hands on them after their baptism. And we can still study Paul's letter to the Christians in Corinth, in which he gave them detailed instructions about this mode of prayer, encouraging them to seek such a gift. So there can be no doubt that praying in tongues has impeccable biblical credentials.

(b) Why was it so valued and thought of as such a precious gift? The answer is that it was believed to be tangible evidence of the complete surrender of the individual personality to God, so that, for the duration of the prayer, even the voice was at the direct disposal of the Holy Spirit. Most often the prayer was—and is today—one of praise and thanksgiving, and like all prayers of gratitude it can strengthen and deepen the relationship of the praying individual with God. But tongues are also used as a form of intercession when it is impossible, humanly speaking, to know just what we should be praying for, what is needed for a particular sufferer or in a confused situation. St Paul wrote to the Romans that in such a case, 'the Spirit himself is pleading for us: and God who searches our inmost being knows what the Spirit means, because he pleads for God's own people in God's own way'. To pray in God's own way—no wonder praying in tongues gives people such great joy! It is as if we lend our voices to Christ for him to intercede. For the same reason tongues are often used as a part of the ministry of healing, thus signifying the complete handing over of the situation and the occasion to God.

(c) However, when praying in public, Paul himself, though highly gifted in tongues, would normally use ordinary speech. 'Suppose you are praising God in the language of inspiration', he wrote, 'how will the plain man who is present be able to say "Amen" to your thanksgiving when he does not know what you are saying?' The gift must always be used with responsible love, for the furtherance of God's kingdom, and this includes making sure that no one is 'left out' or confused or bewildered. For this reason Paul also insisted that if tongues were used publicly they must be accompanied by interpretation, so that the hidden meaning and sense might be made known.

2. MISGIVINGS PEOPLE FEEL

(a) But people can find the gift of interpreting tongues even more of a puzzle than the original prayer! So even with this safeguard it is inevitable that this whole area of prayer should arouse misgivings. To start with, for many of us in this country it can present a cultural problem: it seems so very un-British! The open expression of any deep emotion is traditionally suspect for us, and religious emotion above all. And underlying this is the deeper fear that most of us have of 'letting ourselves go', of losing self-control, or not having total command of any situation. Despite our faith in God, we are like non-swimmers who do not dare to entrust ourselves completely to the water. And of course such fears are not to be entirely dismissed. We do need to be sure that it is God himself to whom we are surrendering, and our conscious intelligence, reason and will are also divine gifts. There is a place for their use in all charismatic groups, so that they may quietly monitor what is going on, lest any errors creep in.

One of these is that we may confuse gifts with goodness, and imagine them to be a proof that we are very close to God. But gifts have no virtue in themselves: it is how they are used that counts. They are given to us as a means of grace for ourselves and others, and rightly used they gradually produce those recognizable fruits of the Spirit which enable us to say of some people whom we meet, that they have been with Jesus. So we need to sit lightly to our gifts of whatever kind. They are at one and the same time very precious and relatively unimportant. The famous pianist Artur Rubinstein said that when he was a little boy he could not understand why people went on and on about his music, when what he wanted them to notice was that he could now jump from the fourth stair! His musicianship just flowed naturally out of him. So if ever we detect any hint of the idea that to have received the gift of tongues makes us in some way 'special'—a member of a spiritual élite—we should be on our guard. Jesus was critical of snobs, spiritual or otherwise, and the spirituality he taught was never in any way pretentious but consisted rather of a simple faithfulness and obedience that was open to all.

(b) Even more seriously, it can happen that charismatic gifts are infiltrated by influences that are not of God. Utterances in tongues may on occasion be the product of an inflated ego or over-stimulated imagination, or, more dangerously, the product of negative elements that are present in the unconscious minds of all human beings—anger, jealousy, lust and fear. Some would want to say firmly that utterances in this latter category are satanic. We could instance the recent sad revelations about some American TV evangelists. But we have to remind ourselves that it is not only 'gifts of the Spirit' that can be abused. Many other forms of prayer, and other spiritual activities, can become distorted. The only reason that special care needs to be exercised in the case of praying in tongues is that the control of the conscious mind has been deliberately removed, so there is a special responsibility of discernment. The test of the true activity of the Holy Spirit is always growth—growth in love and fidelity in the individual and in the community. And another sign that all is well is often that the persons concerned retain a sense of humour and do not take themselves too seriously! We need to remember that we are, all of us, God's fools!

FINALE

St Paul put the whole matter beautifully into perspective when he wrote 'If I speak with the tongues of men or of angels, and have not love, I am a sounding gong or a clanging cymbal'. Whether we praise God in the language of the *Book of Common Prayer*, or in everyday speech, or in tongues, it is what is in our hearts that counts. We all need continually to pray 'Lord, open our lips'. And God will reply to us, as he did to Moses, 'I will be with your mouth and teach you what you shall say'. On our individual pilgrimages, all our lives, at every turn of the road, we too will find that we are given new songs.

9
PRAYER FOR HEALING

Lord, I am not worthy that thou shouldest come under my roof: but speak the word only, and my servant shall be healed.

MATTHEW 8.8 (AV)

The Roman centurion who spoke these words must have been a very remarkable man. For someone in his position to ask Jesus for help was almost the equivalent of an official in Nazi Germany asking for healing from a Jew. Matthew records that Jesus heard him with astonishment: it was clearly an extraordinary and moving encounter for both parties. The way in which he asked, that combination of humility, dignity and faith, can still serve us as a model as we consider how we should pray for healing. In the centurion's request there was no desperation and no doubt, simply an unhurried trust. And the reply of Jesus was equally direct and simple: 'So let it be'.

It is curious, then, that among us the idea of asking God for healing so often arouses fears and misgivings. For, after all, healing is a natural process. Suppose I cut my finger on a sharp-edged grass while gardening and apply a plaster. A few days later I take the plaster off and the skin is as new. Does this frighten me? Do I suspect that there is some supernatural magic at work? Of course not. I take it for granted: it is as simple as that. Healing is entirely in accord with God's purposes and with the way in which we have been made. Jesus positively encouraged people to ask for it. How often he said 'What do you want me to do for you?' There is abundant evidence, too, that he explicitly commanded his disciples to heal, and we have every reason to believe that this command applies to disciples in the twentieth century just as it did in the first.

1. WHAT HEALING IS

How then are we to pray? First, we need to be clear just what it is we are seeking. In the story of the centurion the patient for whom help was sought was a boy who was 'paralysed and racked with pain'. Often people came to Jesus primarily to seek a cure for their physical ailments. But it is clear that Jesus saw before him not just sick bodies but whole people, people with minds and hearts and souls, unique individuals with varying and complex needs. Often, before attending to their physical symptoms, he ministered to their inner dis-ease, their unseen burdens of anxiety and guilt, through the forgiveness of sins. Science today has amply confirmed his deep awareness of the links between our bodies and our minds and emotions. So although Jesus did sometimes speak of healing in terms of 'cure', more often the expression was 'cleansing' or 'making whole'.

It is this wider understanding of healing as 'making whole' that we need to have before us in our prayer. It is something that goes far beyond the 'healthy mind in a healthy body' of the classic ideal. If you and your body, whatever its state, are living together in contented serenity, and with outgoing love, then—even if you have a permanent disability—you are already glowing with health in God's eyes. We have all seen the healing that flows out from such people to others. From this viewpoint, death itself, far from being a disaster, can be seen as the ultimate healing gift—the moment when our redemption is perfected. An ancient Celtic prayer refers to dying as 'being bathed in God's pool'—like the man who was healed in the pool of Bethesda. So that we could say that healing means bringing body, mind and spirit into harmony, and the whole person into harmony with God.

2. HOW WE SHOULD PRAY

When we think of healing in this way, we realize that it is something all human beings need all the time, not just when they are what we call 'ill'. But when there is something wrong with our bodies we are more aware of the need, and often have a greater compulsion to pray. As a rule our prayer will take the form of deep intercession. But now that there is a strong revival of what is known as 'the ministry of healing' in our churches, there may be a more direct involvement, with anointing or the laying on of hands. This may be done by individuals, or in groups, or during a church service, often a Eucharist, which provides an especially beautiful and appropriate setting, since in it we are remembering Our Lord's triumph over suffering and death.

But whenever and however prayer for healing is offered, there are some basic principles which always apply. There must always be careful instruction and preparation beforehand for all who will be involved. We need to monitor all that happens to make sure that the sole intention and result is the manifestation of God's love. It is possible for such ministry to be harmfully distorted into a demonstration of how loving, caring and full of faith *we* are. But we are just there to serve, like the stretcher-bearers in the story. We are those who, as it were, let the sick person down through the roof and lay him at Christ's feet.

Some may be called to a more active role, perhaps giving specific commands in Christ's name, as the apostles did. But they too are well aware that they are simply channels, catalysts if you like, for the interaction that is to take place between God and the sufferer, in which they have no part. When Peter and John healed the crippled beggar at the Beautiful Gate of the Temple, you remember that Peter grasped him by the hand and pulled him up, saying 'In the name of Jesus Christ of Nazareth, walk'. Immediately a crowd gathered, gaping in amazement, in the way in which crowds do when there is drama afoot. Peter's response was unhesitating. 'Why stare at us as if we had made this man walk by some power or godliness of our own?' He had surrendered the whole occasion to God in faith, and his ability to do this arose from a life rooted in prayer.

3. SOME POINTS TO WATCH

(a) We too, if we take healing seriously, must pray ceaselessly that all may be done in love according to God's will. There are certain points that we need to watch with particular care. One of these is the strict avoidance of sensationalism, which can develop especially in the case of healing services with large congregations. It can do much harm, because it distorts what is taking place, introducing notions of 'success' and 'failure', and opening the way for temporary euphoria to masquerade as cure. Why did Jesus so continually shun publicity, asking those he healed to keep it to themselves? Partly, no doubt, for the practical reason that he did not want to attract crowds of people to whom he would not have been able to give the necessary care: there is a lesson for us there. But, even more, because he was scrupulously careful, all his life, about the sort of attention he attracted. It was the goodness of God he wanted to emphasize, not just his miracle-working power. Healing was to be regarded not as 'magic' but as a natural consequence of divine love.

(b) Sometimes, too, misunderstanding may arise when it seems that no healing takes place despite our earnest prayer. It is to avoid such unnecessary disappointment and distress that careful preparation is essential. We should not worry that we do not understand why healing is apparently not given. We may not know, but God does. He may intend for a particular person a marvellous harmony of being which does not require the removal of their cancer or arthritis or the restoration of their failing sight. Or the timing may not be right. If the sufferer has been using his sickness as a way of life, its loss can lead to intense depression: so, deep down, healing will be seen as a threat. In such a case it will always be set aside, but as soon as it can be welcomed it will be there. Or, again, healing may be so gradual as to be imperceptible at first. A woman who had been the victim of appalling cruelty in her earlier life suffered for years from a painful crippling of the whole of the right side of her body. She could move only with difficulty, because, subconsciously, she was defending herself from her hidden angry desire to hit back. After the first seed of healing was planted its full flowering took many months, while her unused muscles were restored by physiotherapy, and she learned to forgive from the heart those who had hurt her so badly. God always knows the right pace.

CONCLUSION

So when we pray for healing we should feel no anxiety about the result. If a matter has been put entirely into God's hands the outcome is never 'wrong'. His light touch of blessing may seem to have left no mark, but it is there. So we can intercede in absolute trust, as the centurion did. God's mercy and love are great enough to reach out to us in all our self-centredness, sickness and pain, to make us whole, and to preserve our bodies, and souls, unto everlasting life.

10
PRAYING IN ORDINARINESS

I have come that men may have life, and may have it in all its fullness.

JOHN 10.10 (NEB)

A few years ago I met a woman in her early sixties who began to tell me something about her life. She said that she had always felt overshadowed, and that nothing had ever worked out entirely right for her. She had made an unsuitable marriage in order to get away from home, and when it ended she was left with a handicapped child to look after. Later she had taken a job in which she was never really a success, although she could not say it had been a disaster. She had kept going, she was quite comfortably off, and she had one happily married daughter and the joy of a new grandchild. I suppose she had not really undergone more of life's pain than most people. But I found it very moving to hear her say 'I'd like to live before I die'.

Ordinary life for this woman was a sort of perpetual dull ache. She had not lost her faith. She would never say that she had been abandoned by God, but at the same time he was not near enough to give her any real joy. It was not easy for her to pray.

For a great many people, I think, ordinariness is like that. For others, it may mean resigning themselves to a humdrum routine in which they feel bored and imprisoned. But the difficulty of praying in such a mood is that if we are only half alive then God can seem only half alive too. Strong emotions such as grief and despair often drive us into God's arms, as they drove the prodigal son into his father's. It was the elder brother in that story who lived the routine life of unremarkable prosperity and comfort. I cannot help suspecting that he was a bit jealous, not only of the homecoming celebrations, but also of the fleshpots and the goings-on in the far country. Like the woman I mentioned, was he also crying out inside, 'I'd like to live before I die'? And he had not managed, either, to learn about forgiving love. Ordinariness is not always very easy to manage, is it? It is not always easy to pray that vital prayer of repentance out of ordinariness, when we are not conscious of having committed any spectacular sins. But, of course, we do not know the end of the story. Was the elder brother, reaffirmed in his father's love, finally able to ask for forgiveness, too?

1. BEING OURSELVES

So we have located two of the difficulties about praying in ordinariness. It is not easy to repent. And it is not easy to have a deep sense of the reality of God. There is a tendency for us to comfort ourselves at such times by persuading ourselves that to be dull and bored is somehow virtuous. Well, of course we all have dull times in our lives and it is certain that by God's grace they can be creatively used. Just hanging on in faith can be very important and steadiness can become a wonderful quality of committed loyalty. But to be half alive is not a virtue in itself, and if we find ourselves persistently remaining in that state then I think we have to look rather honestly at the ordinariness we are stuck with, and ask ourselves if we are as willing to be changed by God as we think we are. Dullness can easily become a cloak for apathy, laziness or fear. We feel safer when we stay within familiar boundaries and avoid the risk of moving on. Ordinariness then becomes a state which we ourselves prefer and choose. It is, in a way, a defence against God.

(a) What is the answer for us? How can we be helped to move on? First, we can ask ourselves whether we are praying in reality. By praying in reality I mean exactly that: saying something to God that is completely real. It is so easy to spend our prayer time struggling to conjure up good and holy feelings. We give thanks to God for things for which we are not grateful, because we have been taught that we ought to be grateful. We say, 'I feel hurt' when what we really mean is, 'I feel angry'. Admitting to God that actually we intensely dislike certain people is a necessary first step towards learning to love them. To leave out that step, to pretend to ourselves that we love our enemies because we know we ought to, is a subterfuge that may deceive us, but God knows the truth of it. And as soon as unreality creeps in, true dialogue is at an end.

Last Christmas a friend told me about an encounter she had just had with a small boy. She had been told that he had taken part in a nativity play performed by the infant class at his school. 'What part did you play?' she asked him. The answer was 'A hay bale'! Somewhat taken aback, but wanting to be kind, she then asked him if he'd had to say anything. He looked at her with withering contempt. 'Hay doesn't speak!' he said, and walked off. Well, I am sure that God is just as quick to spot our attempts to humour him as that little boy was. But, unlike the little boy, he goes on patiently waiting for a spark of authenticity to break through. It is we who find ourselves becoming apathetic and bored.

(b) There is another aspect of praying in reality which is worth bearing in mind. It is that we should discover not only our weaknesses, but also what it is in us that gives us spontaneous joy and delight. And if these inner springs seem to be in conflict with what we think God is telling us to do, then this is a situation we should look at carefully. It is not for nothing that each of us has been created as a unique individual. And if we deny our own most joyful inner responses we need to be sure that it is God himself who is asking us to deny them, and not some quite unnecessary guilt or fear. Recently a young man said to me that he could not understand why people found it so difficult to recognize God's will: we had only to discover what *we* wanted and then do the opposite! Well, of course the rebuking voice of conscience is often truly the voice of God. But sometimes, too, it may be the voice of an authoritarian parent or teacher from long ago, who is still saying, 'Don't do that!' deep inside us, creating an obstacle to the free flowing of God's grace. Often we keep ourselves in a prison from which we will not allow the Holy Spirit to liberate us. So if we feel that we are missing something, that our lives are ordinary, dull, boring even, and that we ourselves are dull, boring people, could it be that we are not allowing ourselves to be authentic, to respond to God as we actually are?

I like the story of the college principal who was interviewing a new student and asked her what she wanted to be. 'I just want to be myself!', the luckless girl replied. 'Come, come, my dear', was the sharp retort, 'I think we can do a little better than that!' But the interesting thing is that they were *both* right. When we are willing to be completely ourselves before God, then it is that his grace can get to us and make us 'better', sometimes changing us beyond our imaginings.

2. THE AUTHENTICITY OF JESUS

Look, for a moment, at the example of Our Lord. One of the most noticeable facts about the life of Jesus is the complete authenticity of everything he said or did. He made a clear distinction between being 'nice' and being good. Was he always doing what other people wanted? We all know that he was not, and that the gospels present a very different figure. Jesus took his stand on those words he is recorded as having uttered at the age of twelve, 'I must be about my Father's business'. Did he require others to tell him what this was? How hopelessly they would have got it wrong. How hopelessly they *did* get it wrong, as the endless criticisms of him show. 'Why does he eat with sinners? Why doesn't he fast? Why doesn't he keep the Law of Moses? Why does he allow that woman to waste that ointment on him? How dare he heal on the Sabbath?', and so on. Yet the result of Jesus placing himself in God's hands utterly, and following his own path, a path fully known only to God, was not selfishness, but a life of steadfast, selfless love, unaffected by the praise or blame of men.

So that being authentic, being real, paradoxically does not mean just overriding others, arrogantly insisting on our own way. Perhaps we have noticed that one result of people becoming more aware of their own inner selves is that they also become more aware of God. They are more able to respond to him. They are also more able to respond to other people. They become not more callous and arrogant but quite the reverse—more truly humble, more sensitive, and, yes, slowly and gradually more selfless. This is the true, saintly ordinariness of those who are content simply to be what God makes them, not the dull, deadening ordinariness of those who cling to a mask through pride or fear.

FINALE

So let us pray in our ordinariness, in the midst of our humdrum, routine lives, that God will wake us, shake us, and reveal to us what it is in us that is authentic, the true self that he sees and loves. Our Lord has made his intention plain for us. 'I have come that men may have life, and may have it in all its fullness.' No human being ever was or could be ordinary or boring to God.

11
PRAYING IN CONFUSION

O send out thy light and thy truth, that they may lead me.

PSALM 43.3 (BCP)

At least once a week, and very likely every day, we all pray the Lord's Prayer, and say 'Thy will be done'. The idea of doing God's will is central to our Christian commitment. It was central to the commitment of Jesus. He had no sense at all of 'doing his own thing'. 'I am not myself the source of the words I speak to you: It is the Father who dwells in me doing his own work.' At first sight it seems, too, that he had no difficulty in knowing what God's will was. He was able to respond to unexpected situations with confidence. How different it is for us. We may sincerely want to do God's will: but what is it? Sometimes we want to cry out that he is not being fair. Here we are in confusion, longing to know what we should do for the best, but still being left in darkness. We do not know whether to move house or not; whether to turn a blind eye to the goings-on of that rebellious adolescent or toughen up on him; whether to have our lonely, demanding mother-in-law to live with us or resist it for the sake of the harmony of our marriage.

And that is not all. If we look at those of our fellow human beings who are able to state confidently that God has revealed his will to them, that they have a word from the Lord, or whatever phrase they use, then we come up against another problem. These very certain people do not always agree with each other. Some passionately believe that God is telling them that women should be ordained to the priesthood. Some believe the exact opposite. We have to admit that the lack of clear answers to our prayers for guidance is baffling. If God really wants us to do his will, why, oh why, does he not show us plainly what it is?

1. JESUS FACING UNCERTAINTY

In trying to find an answer there is no better place to begin than the gospels. Is it true that Jesus never suffered any doubt or bewilderment? What really happened in the wilderness? We are told that Jesus was there for forty days, which is a symbolic Jewish way of saying that he was there for quite a long time. Was it not indeed a period of confusion, when he had to sort himself out? Note that this was not a question of whether or not he should commit himself to doing God's will. That decision had already been taken. He had already been publicly baptized and had received the gift of the Holy Spirit for his life's work. But he did not know for certain how to begin. There were many alluring possibilities, which were presented to him as temptations. For instance, Jesus was aware by now that he had the charisma of a natural leader and that he had the ability to lead his countrymen to freedom, vindicating the honour of the true God against the false gods of their conquerors. Would not this be a fine thing to do in God's service? The prophets had left the role of the Messiah very ambiguous. Many of them certainly saw the saviour of the race in this light. Very few equated the Messiah with the suffering servant image, the man who would be despised and rejected, whose kingdom was not of this world. So what was Jesus to do and be for God? The discernment of his Father's will was a costly struggle for him. He did not eat or sleep and was afterwards exhausted.

There are many other instances where we can see that his decisions were not entirely effortless and spontaneous. There was the occasion when he spent the whole night in prayer before choosing the Twelve. And there is Gethsemane. Was this death a nonsense, an arrogant courting of martyrdom which should have been avoided or postponed? Was it a senseless cutting off of his work half-accomplished? Looking at the way the disciples behaved, we could not say they inspired confidence as being fully trained, could we? Or was this death, with all its agony, truly the will of God? It seems that Jesus was no stranger to our human pain, nor to our human uncertainty.

2. CONFUSION AS A THRESHOLD

(a) The fact is that it is almost impossible for us to move forward without going through a period of confusion. While we go on in the same old ways we more or less know the answers, but as soon as one factor is altered we feel lost. To take a trivial example, think what it is like when your tennis coach tries to change your serve. Your old serve may not have been all that stylish, but at least it went in. But now you are in a transition stage, where you cannot do your old serve, and you cannot do your new one. It seems a backward step, but when you have persevered and established the new serve you can see that the confusion was a necessary part of the process. Perhaps it is very uncomfortable for a chrysalis to be neither a caterpillar nor a butterfly! We have to remember that our feelings, although they are important in other ways, are very poor indicators of our spiritual state. When we are confused we long for our former peace and certainty. We feel 'worse', but this does not mean that we *are* worse: often we are in a state of grace and going forward. Confusion is a threshold, and if we can see it in this way we may even be able to give thanks for it. Now I see in a glass, darkly, but then face to face.

(b) There is one necessary warning, though. Confusion is not meant to be a permanent state. If we try to cling to it, actively resisting clarification, it may be that, uncomfortable though it is, we are actually preferring it to facing unpalatable truth. So if our uneasiness continues over a long period, despite our prayers for guidance, it may be that we should seek help in discerning what we are trying to hide from. This is poignantly illustrated in Graham Greene's novel *The Heart of the Matter*. The chief character, Scobie, is trapped in an impossible, exhausting marriage. The conflict he experiences between his pity for his wife and his guilt feelings about her, on the one hand, and his longing to be free of it all on the other, totally disrupts his inner peace. Then, almost by accident, he launches into an affair with a young woman who is a war victim, the survivor of a ship lost at sea. Now he has two conflicting responsibilities. Despairing of ever resolving his confusion or discovering what God's will could be in such a situation, he commits suicide.

Every day during those last months Scobie had prayed 'O Lamb of God, that takest away the sins of the world, grant us thy peace'. And yet he could not allow God to give him the peace for which he longed. He was trapped in confusion by his fear: fear of hurting either of the women, though he was, of course, all the time hurting both; fear of entrusting either of them to God; fear that he himself had transgressed so utterly that he was beyond the pale of God's mercy. He could neither face the truth himself nor allow either his wife or his mistress to do so. Even the pain of death was preferable to the pain of allowing the situation to be faced and clarified. So the confusion which might have been a threshold of repentance and a means of growth for all three people involved, became literally a death trap. Yet we can feel compassion for Scobie. To hand a situation over to God completely, and to be willing to face the consequences of so doing, can require much courage and trust.

3. LETTING GOD FIND THE ANSWERS

For however sincerely we pray that God's will may be done, a part of us continues to believe that it is up to us to find the solution to our problems. When we think we are praying for guidance, we are often actually spending our prayer time frantically explaining and re-explaining our problem to God. We try to discover what his will is by putting up various alternative policies from A to E and asking him to indicate his preferences. But he invariably comes up with solution F, something we would never even have thought of, a new angle that takes us completely by surprise. How often God must long to shout to us 'Just shut up for a moment and let me get a word in edgeways'. Be still and know that I am God. Be still and trust. As often as we can we must put the arguments, the fuss and bustle, aside. We need to come before God empty-handed, with no answers, no policies, no solutions, and simply focus our thoughts on God himself. After a while we may find that, mysteriously, there is a difference. The problem may not have changed, but we have. God has changed us, marginally perhaps, but even a small change is a vitally new factor. We have a slightly different perception, a little more confidence, a little more hope. And if this way of praying sounds like an evasion, a recipe for doing nothing, I can only say that it does not work out like that in practice. The more we have attended quietly upon God, the greater the likelihood that a decision will come spontaneously from us at the moment when this has become necessary. And then, even if subsequently we have doubts about the rightness of what we have decided, we must trust. God can bring good even out of our errors. He can infuse every situation with his presence and his love will not fail. If once we can accept this, is it not an unbelievable release and relief?

FINALE

St Paul wrote 'They that wait upon the Lord shall renew their strength'—not they who work out ten fresh solutions to their problems every day before breakfast. It is God, not us, who will be wise. O send out thy light and thy truth, that they may lead us. And help us truly to say 'Thy will be done'.

12
PRAYING IN LONELINESS

'And be assured, I am with you always, to the end of time.'
MATTHEW 28.20 (NEB)

In a moving short poem the Welsh priest-poet, R. S. Thomas, imagines himself having to write a single word to describe what it is like to be a human being. The word that appears on the blank page is 'lonely', and this is such an unwelcome insight that he instinctively moves to rub it out:

my hand moved
to erase it: but the voices
of all those waiting at life's
window cried out loud 'It is true'.

Loneliness is an inescapable part of the human condition and afflicts all of us at some time in our lives, though in varying degrees. There are pockets of aloneness in even the happiest partnerships, and when these end there is the unbearable ache of bereavement or separation. Many thousands, too, have to endure the chronic pain of permanent loneliness because they are unable to form relationships; or because they fail to achieve a particular relationship—marriage, for instance—on which they have set their heart. The pain is made much worse by the expectations of society, the continual pressure to make us believe that the only possible happiness or fulfilment in our lives lies in having an intimate relationship, usually sexual; or in being admired and sought after within a social group. All other ways of living are branded as second-rate. It is no wonder that when we are lonely, for whatever reason, we often compound our misery by seeing ourselves and our lives as failures. Then we may become bitter and resentful because of what life has done to us, or depressed and guilty because we think our isolation is due to some flaw in ourselves for which we are to blame. For Christians there is often the added guilt of knowing that Christ 'ought' to be sufficient for all our need, yet being unable to feel it. And the cumulative effect of all these painful feelings—isolation, anger, depression, guilt—is often to make prayer difficult if not impossible. So when we are lonely we may end up isolated not only from our fellow human beings but also—so it feels—from God.

1. HEALING OUR LONELINESS

(a) Of course, this is not always the case. Many people who have suffered bereavement have had a certainty that God is with them, even though this knowledge does not at the time relieve their pain. But when loneliness is not due to some specific happening—exile, imprisonment, separation, loss—but is a permanent bleak feature of the landscape of our inner lives, we may have an even harder road to travel. If we try to talk to people who are suffering in this way about the constant companionship of God, we may even make things worse for them by increasing their guilt. They may be sincere Christians who believe with their minds that God is love, and would give this reassurance to others, but cannot accept it for themselves. Often they live in a perpetual numbing despair, which communicates itself to those who try to help them. They may continue to pray, and the prayer may continue to be a desperate plea, 'Lord, send me a friend, a companion, a wife or husband, a child'. But the prayer is apparently not answered, and they remain alone.

So it may be time to change the prayer. If love seems to be something of a 'no-go area' for us, we may need to approach God through another of his attributes, truth. Often in my life I have been grateful to Reinhold Niebuhr for his famous prayer 'God, give us grace to accept with serenity the things that cannot be changed, courage to change the things that should be changed, and the wisdom to distinguish the one from the other'. Lord, hold me to the truth and do not let me wriggle away, however great my pain. 'O send out thy light and thy truth that they may lead me.' For often we are unconsciously clinging to our loneliness for fear of further rejection, which may painfully emphasize yet again our own shortcomings, or as an angry gesture against those who have rejected us in the past. And if this is the case we are at one and the same time asking God to help us and rejecting his help. But if we can find the courage to put ourselves entirely into God's hands, he will faithfully guide us. He may gradually heal our memories directly through the channel of our prayer. Or he may guide us to seek help from another human being—a priest, counsellor, or doctor—or through the ministry of spiritual healing. The guidance may come as a quiet, rational decision to seek such help, or as a compulsion because our distress becomes so acute that we realize there is no alternative. But having made such a decision we often experience some immediate relief because we are no longer running away.

This was brought home to me a few years ago in a vivid dream in which I was on a railway platform where some terrible disaster had occurred. In panic I joined the crowd who were rushing, screaming, towards the exit. Then suddenly it came to me that if I did not turn round and face whatever had happened, I would be afraid for ever. I began to elbow my way back again through the jostling mob. Instantly my fear vanished and I felt calm and resolute and ready to help. At this point I woke, but the memory of the transformation remained with me. So if we can pray in our loneliness, 'Lord, if there is something you want to show me, give me the courage to face the truth and to know that I shall find you there too', we may begin at once to feel that we are on firmer ground.

(b) However, we know that there are many members of the human family who experience loneliness all their lives. Does this mean that they are failures, that their lives are completely invalidated? Most emphatically it does not. God's purposes can be carried out in every life that is offered to him. Many of the world's greatest geniuses—Beethoven, Van Gogh, William Blake—have been intensely lonely people. The lonely, the depressed, have their own special qualities and insights, and the gospels show that they made a special claim on Christ's heart. I have a friend who is a severely afflicted manic-depressive. I have seen her at times when she has felt cut off from all human contact, restrained in a high-sided cot in a psychiatric hospital, suffering a bleak agony of isolation. Yet all who know her are aware of the underlying continuity of her courage and goodness: beneath the grotesque distortions her innermost soul continues to glow. For many, loneliness is less dramatic. Indeed, part of its pain is that no one else really knows the extent of the suffering, it is hidden away. But it is known to God, and if we openly share it with him in prayer, there are many paths along which, through his grace, we may be safely led.

2. SHARING OUR LONELINESS WITH GOD

(a) One requirement may be that we learn to love God for his own sake, and not merely as a substitute for another human being. How could God ever be a 'substitute' for anything? It is as if we said to him, 'O God, I am really looking for someone else, but perhaps you will do instead'! We would not easily find many of our fellow humans who would be willing to be our companions on those terms! But if we truly turn to him we find that our attitude to our loneliness begins to change. In some way that we do not fully understand, we find that we can bear it, after all. Monks and nuns who have voluntarily embraced the celibate life often evince a marvellous contentment and joy, but many of them would say that they have remained aware of a human ache which all their lives never quite disappears. They do not *want* it to disappear. They are not trying to escape from the human condition, but to allow God's grace to permeate it entirely, so that both joy and pain are infused with his presence. As Christians, we are not asked to *suppress* our human longings. But what we can pray for, and receive, is the sufficient grace of God transforming our need. For slowly we begin to see that our actual 'need' is not at all the same as our idealized dreams. We begin to understand how precious our daily bread is, and how much security we can derive from the regularity with which we receive it. We may even discover that our very best human companion is—ourselves! Me, myself and God can make a very good trio, and not necessarily a selfish one, either. So our prayer becomes 'O God, help me to love you for yourself alone, and be with me in my human need every day of my life'.

(b) This whole idea of not looking for substitutes but valuing not only God, but each and every person, animal, object and event for what they are in themselves, is a far-reaching concept which, once it is grasped, has huge healing potential for us in our loneliness. We should not be afraid to say that this absorbed attention is a true form of love. So can we allow ourselves to receive even from casual contacts what they have of value for us and not despise them because they are not the close relationships we could prefer? Can we allow Mozart to be Mozart whatever our situation? Can a sunset be just as beautiful when we are alone? The answer is, of course, yes, but it is an answer we find extraordinarily difficult to give. Shakespeare expressed this so exactly in his sonnet on loneliness with the line 'With what I most enjoy contented least'. At a time of sadness in my own life I found that I felt worse in beautiful surroundings and had more peace in the concrete ugliness of the inner city, living a few minutes' walk from Spaghetti Junction. There, where I had no expectations of delight, I found amid the noise and litter a symbolism which matched my mood. But God in his mercy preserved the full beauty of the countryside for me until the day when I was able to allow him to restore it to me in all its glory. So in our loneliness we also need to pray that we may have the truthfulness to contain our pain in the area to which it belongs, and not allow it to rob us of all joy. 'Counting our blessings' is not an exercise in facile optimism but a demanding encounter with truth.

(c) 'O send out thy light and thy truth that they may lead me.' This must be our ceaseless prayer. For by means of it God can lead us to a moment that will transform our lives. We have been taught since childhood that 'What can't be cured must be endured'. But the moment of revelation comes when we perceive the possibility of changing this to 'What can't be cured must be *hallowed*'. If our loneliness cannot be altered then we are being called by God to be alone. It is our vocation, not our failure. In one of his greatest poems Philip Larkin writes of our inner compulsions being first recognized and then 'robed as destinies'. The suffering which we have always thought of as an affliction which prevents us from living becomes the very substance of life, that through which God will reveal to us his glory. Gonville ffrench-Beytagh, a lifelong depressive, has written 'You begin not to dread depression. You know it will come, for that is your lot: but there is the knowledge that you will find God afterwards.' The psalmist says 'Darkness is no darkness with thee, but the night is as clear as the day: darkness and light to thee are both alike'. Darkness and light co-exist in us, and God is in both. Christ understood loneliness, and so too, perhaps, does God, continually experiencing the rejection of his love. So we are not cut off from God, but sharing in his aloneness. Slowly we discover that Christ's promise, 'I am with you always', is as true for us as for others. We are no longer failures. And because we have so earnestly sought the God who is Truth as well as Love, we can have the certainty that we shall receive the welcome given to all true pilgrims. One day, as for Mr Valiant-for-Truth, not only the trumpets but the whole orchestra of heaven will sound for us on the other side.

13
PRAYING IN DOUBT

Lord, I believe : help thou mine unbelief.

MARK 9.24 (AV)

Once, many years ago, I was called upon to administer a test to a group of students. It was supposed to help them in their choice of a career by indicating whether they were outgoing, reflective, practical, and so on. The answers had to be sorted into three categories: yes, no, and lies! A few of the questions were designed to test their self-confidence by revealing whether they dared to admit that they were sometimes less than perfect. One of these questions was 'Have you ever told a lie?' No one can truthfully answer 'no' to that! We ought perhaps to have similar misgivings if we find ourselves saying 'no' to the question 'Have you ever had any doubts?' because never having doubts may not be a sign of faith, but of fear. We have not dared to think for fear of what might we discover. Socrates said that the unexamined life is not worth living, and similarly we could say that unexamined faith is not worth holding, because it is not yet absolute faith. It has not stood the test of life, but has dodged it. Our 'doubts' may be evidence of a profound commitment to serve God with our whole being, including our minds. So the opposite of faith is not doubt, but the sort of unreflective credulity in which we cling to our own comfort and security above all.

For, of course, doubt is not comfortable, and it often catches us unawares. In the very act of praying, we may suddenly find our situation ridiculous. Here we are kneeling and talking to—whom? Is there really anyone listening? Or we may have doubts which grow more slowly, when some doctrine or tenet of the Church which satisfies our hearts seems not to satisfy our minds, or vice versa. Then often it is hard to pray because we feel hypocritical. We may also fear to be open with our fellow Christians in case they are shocked and condemn us. Because the nature of doubt is so little understood, it is true that this does happen. A few years ago a university lecturer in theology caused a stir by saying that he had lost his faith. He was pilloried in some sections of the press as if he had committed heinous sin. But when sincere pilgrims are assailed by doubt they deserve not our condemnation but our understanding. Even the faith of Jesus failed momentarily on the cross. Our prayer must be that God in his mercy will open up fresh paths for them—and, if need be, for us.

1. EXAMINING OUR DOUBTS

(a) For sometimes, when we doubt, it may be that we are being challenged, not to surrender God, but to surrender a particular image of him which we ourselves have made. Our human picture of God can never be the whole truth. None of us would claim perfectly to understand the mind of Christ. Even St John, who had been so close to Jesus, wrote later that 'no man has seen God at any time'. So when we feel we are losing faith it may be that just the opposite is the case, and that we are being led into a faith that is deeper and more mature.

Let us take a seventeenth-century example. Before that time the accepted picture of the universe showed not only where heaven was located but also how God could control the movements of the planets whilst residing there. When Galileo discovered through his observation of the moons of Jupiter that this cosmic structure did not exist, he was condemned by a terrified Church for displacing God. In Brecht's play *Galileo* there is a scene where Galileo and his assistant are alone together at the moment of this discovery. His friend breaks into Galileo's jubilation by saying:

> 'But God, where is God? Where is God in your universe?'
> 'Am I a theologian? I'm a mathematician.'
> 'First and foremost, you are a man. And I ask you, where is God?'

There is a long pause, and then Galileo replies, 'In us, or nowhere'.

Was God displaced or damaged by the truth that we cannot assign to him a geographical location? Quite the reverse. We no longer have any need to think of him as being 'above the bright blue sky'. In fact we see that such an idea actually diminishes him. We have become aware of the divine mystery of God's all-pervading presence. Of course, not all our new insights are true, but we can be sure that those which are mere human aberrations will eventually fall away. 'The light shines on in the dark, and the darkness has never overcome it.' So doubts, like everything else in our life that gives us pain, are not to be feared but to be lived through and continually offered to God in prayer. Above all, we should not rush to condemn ourselves or abandon our entire pilgrimage in sudden panic. We must go on praying as steadily as we can, and wait patiently for further inner conviction as to what, if anything, we ought to do. God will not easily let us go! Even our doubt can be creatively used for our spiritual growth.

(b) But at such times we do also need to ask ourselves whether we are allowing our minds completely to dominate the scene. If the seventeenth-century church had been guided by its experience of the presence of God as well as by logic it would not have been so afraid of scientific truth. Now, as it happens, since the development of quantum theory, physicists too have had to admit the existence of the unknowable, of mystery. Living with mystery and living with doubt are two sides of the same coin. We cannot argue our way into faith, and if we ignore our instincts and intuitions and feelings we are responding to God with only part of ourselves. Our minds on their own can lead us into untruth rather than into truth. As the hymn says, 'experience will decide'. If we continually seek God's presence in prayer, we will find that we can be far more tolerant of our doubts, seeing them as the will o' the wisps they often are.

2. LEAVING GOD IN ANGER

But if we are tempted to take leave of God, not through the genuine searchings of the pilgrim, but through bitterness and anger, that is a different case. We often hear people say that they have lost their faith because of the death of a child, or the prolonged pain of a loved one, or because they cannot equate suffering such as that endured in the famine-stricken areas of Africa with the existence of a God of love. Either God is powerless, or his nature is one of callous indifference. In either case they want no more to do with him. Such a reaction is natural at first. But to take permanent leave of God in this way is to be like an angry child saying 'All right, then, I won't play'. We have become trapped in an image of God which we need to surrender. Before Christ came, the emphasis was, indeed, on the sheer physical omnipotence of God. He was, above all, that being who creates and destroys, who controls the destinies of men and nations, intervening by powerful acts to judge or save. But Christ gave us a wider interpretation of the nature of God's power. It is not just an infinitely magnified version of what we think of as power—the power to compel and control. In Jesus we see someone who was handed over to the power of others, who endured mockery, pain and death with unshakeable dignity and love. Did he ever promise his disciples that they would be spared suffering? After his death they had, if anything, more than their share. But they still rejoiced in the overwhelming gift of his presence. It is this presence, this love, in which ultimately we put our trust—not just the love which intervenes to remove or avert ills, but the love which enables us to transcend them. So if, at a time of angry doubt, we can find within ourselves even a spark of desire to believe that 'it's love that makes the world go round', we must cherish it with all our might. We must pray that God will not let us wriggle free of this truth, no matter how great our pain. If we can surrender our bitterness, even for a fleeting moment, Christ will be instantly at our side. Our moment of peace may not last, but it will be enough to show us where our true path lies, and to give us the courage to go on.

3. STAYING WITH GOD

For even though it may seem that, for whatever reason, we have temporarily lost God, we may still be able to keep faith with his substance—his attributes of love, holiness and truth. Many people who have clung to these have later found to their surprise that they were clinging to God after all—just as people who offer hospitality to strangers may, as St Paul says, entertain angels without knowing it. There is a moving passage in the fourth gospel where Jesus turns to the Twelve, after many of his disciples have deserted him, and asks them 'Do you also want to leave me?' Simon Peter replies 'Lord, to whom shall we go?' What light can we see anywhere which can compare with the light that shines from the Christ-figure? If it is all too good to be true, it is still the highest good we can see. So if there is nowhere else to go, let us simply stay where we are. Let us wait patiently, praying in the rags of our faith. Lord, I believe: help thou mine unbelief. And, sooner or later, it will mysteriously be made known to us that our prayer is acceptable, and has been heard.

14

PRAYING IN PAIN

Out of the deep have I called unto thee, O Lord: Lord, hear my voice.

PSALM 130.1 (BCP)

I think we would all have to agree that pain is one of the most inescapably real experiences of our lives. There are many things that we can gloss over or ignore, but pain is not one of them. Whether it is extreme physical pain, or agony of mind, or the dereliction of despair, it demands our attention. It makes us aware, as nothing else can, of the fragility of our minds and hearts and bodies. We often say, in the grief and shock of bereavement or some other sudden catastrophe, that we have been 'knocked for six'. A woman whose husband had been killed in a road accident wrote some weeks afterwards: 'I feel that I am floundering in unfamiliar waters'. Our illusion of self-sufficiency, of our competence to deal with our emotions, is swept away. C.S. Lewis said, 'All my little happinesses look like broken toys'. They reflect back to us the brokenness of our hearts.

How strong does our faith have to be to protect us from such shattering pain? The answer is that this is something no faith can do. Pain is pain, and it is painful. This causes much puzzlement among Christians who often misunderstand the role of faith, and feel that it should act as a sort of anaesthetic. Did it for Jesus? In Gethsemane we see him sweating in terror at the thought of a cruel and imminent death. And on the cross his pain—both mental and physical—was so great that he cried out, using the remembered words of an ancient song, that God had forsaken him. No, faith is more like an invisible rope that holds us as the avalanche sweeps by. It holds us even as we are crying out to God that it is *not* holding: we do not see the other end securely held in his hand. But the very act of crying out keeps it in place. As we know, many people who do not normally pray at all, and are not sure that they have any belief, do shout out to whatever God there is, whenever they are in danger or desperate need. And although some will immediately feel ashamed of their weakness, and stifle the cry at source, for others it becomes a turning point in their lives. In William Golding's novel *Free Fall*, a man who has been a prisoner of war looks back on such a moment in the camp:

> My cry for help was the cry of the rat when the terrier shakes it, a hopeless sound. . . . But the very act of crying out *changed the thing that cried.*

To admit honestly that we are in need, in some mysterious way allows all the sources of strength latent within our own personalities to be gathered up, and, above and beyond this, it makes accessible to us another, profounder strength, derived from a source that, as yet, we may not even be able to recognize as divine.

1. IS OUR PRAYER HEARD?

(a) Curiously, lesser degrees of pain may be more dangerous for us because they leave us able to believe that we are totally in control of our lives. We can side-step, evade or stifle our suffering instead of going through it to God. We never make that irresistible cry *de profundis* which summons him right into the centre of our being. Yet, at the time, even when we do pray for help, we may not at first be aware of any answering response. C. S. Lewis wrote, in his moving analysis of bereavement, *A Grief Observed*:

> When you are happy you will be—or so it feels—welcomed with open arms. But go to him when your need is desperate, when all other help is in vain, and what do you find? A door slammed in your face, and a sound of bolting and double-bolting on the inside. After that, silence.

(b) A Bishop has related that after his wife's death all the glib words of comfort that he had so frequently offered to others utterly failed him. In the end it was in a book of psychology that he found some reassurance and relief, because it offered explanations for the unexpected and terrible range of emotions that had overtaken him—the anger, guilt, anxiety, lostness and despair. In the first weeks he would have said, with the psalmist, 'Oh my God, I cry in the day-time, but thou hearest not: and in the night-season also I take no rest'. And yet—the days passed, and still he survived. What is more, he went on praying. Why? It is the experience of thousands that, despite God's apparent deafness, we *do* go on praying. It seems absurd. What is it that holds us there? Gradually, very gradually, it dawns upon us that God has *not* let us go, that all this time he has been, as it were, praying in us, when of ourselves we could do nothing. Through those intolerable days, and even worse nights, the everlasting arms have been beneath us all the time.

2. THE MEANING OF SUFFERING

During the first tentative weeks or months after some great trauma—or if our pain is chronic, often for much longer periods—there are many apparently unanswerable questions with which we tend to torment ourselves. One of them is the classic 'Why?' Why are you doing this to me, Lord—or to my partner, my friend, my child? Why should there be such suffering in the world at all? What is its meaning, its purpose? It is a valid question for us to put to God when we pray in anger and bewilderment at our own or someone else's undeserved pain. We could bear it all better, we feel, if only God would show us that there is some *point* to it all.

We can see, of course, that there was purpose and meaning in the suffering of Jesus. He died that we might go to heaven, making a full, perfect and sufficient sacrifice for the sins of the whole world. But we do not as a rule die *for* anything. We just die. I believe that we must dare to say it: often the suffering of humanity is, *in itself*, meaningless. If we tried to tell one of the victims of the Ethiopian famines that there is some hidden purpose in his or her suffering, I believe we should deserve all the anger we should undoubtedly provoke. Is it not, perhaps, more true that suffering is simply a fact, and that *meaning* lies in the people who suffer? Many people besides Jesus suffered crucifixion or other cruel deaths. What of Stephen, the first martyr, pleading as he died for forgiveness for those who were stoning him? What of the hundreds of men and women who walked upright into the gas chambers of Auschwitz with the Shema Yisrael or the Lord's Prayer on their lips? We revere these people, but we do not worship them or think their deaths redemptive. The 'meaning' of the suffering of the cross lay in the person of Jesus: it was God who died.

So though we may see no purpose in the suffering of those around us, we do see meaning and value in the sufferers. We believe that at the heart and core of each is an intrinsic, unquenchable inner meaning, something that transcends animal humanity, something that is touched by the divine. 'I have called you Sons.' So we offer our prayer for those in pain, not only in pity and compassion, but in reverence and awe,—yes, even when they seem to be reduced almost to nothing. Viktor Frankl, an Austrian psychiatrist who was himself a survivor of Auschwitz, once memorably wrote:

> An incurably psychotic individual may lose his usefulness but yet retain the dignity of a human being. This is my credo. Without it I would not think it worth while to be a psychiatrist. For whose sake? Just for the sake of the damaged brain machine which cannot be repaired? No. Man is more than psyche. The innermost core of the patient's personality is not even touched by his illness. That is his soul.

3. CREATIVE SUFFERING

And so, in a curious way, we are each enabled to impart to our suffering a unique individual meaning. If we accept it without evasion, if we drain the cup, it is somehow, by God's grace, transformed. Our continual prayer that we may do God's will, within each and every situation, changes our suffering from waste into a source of new life. The psalmist sang of those 'who going through the vale of misery use it for a well'. It is rare for anyone who has passed through great suffering to be able to explain just how they were enabled to do so, or to identify the moment when they began to understand that it was changing them, that after the initial shock of separation it was actually bringing them nearer—much nearer—to God. They can only say that the experience has given them a new, inalienable certainty and trust. Faith that has been tested in such fire will never be lost. So pain has been robbed of much of its terror. In T.S. Eliot's play *Murder in the Cathedral*, the Archbishop says to his terrified companions, as his assassins hammer on the door, 'I am not in danger: only near to death'. We know that, ultimately, all will be well.

And I expect we have all noticed another glorious fact. People who have been through great pain and have emerged on the far side, with a new wholeness of being, wear this experience unmistakably, like a badge, so that others who are still suffering recognize it instantly. They know where they can go for understanding and support. It works almost like a mason's handshake. In my work as a counsellor I see this again and again. Those who have known what it is to pass through the dark valley, and emerge into the light, now carry this light for others. It is the light of indestructible love, which can never be put out.

So our prayer 'out of the deep' is the most crucial we shall ever make. A young priest whose two-year-old son had to have surgery for a malignant brain tumour, in a desperate attempt to save his life, told me of his feelings as he sat with the child in the hour preceding the operation. The night before, he had been reading St John's account of the passion of Jesus, who had allowed himself to be handed over into the power of those who sought his death. But, in truth, in surrendering all his independence and initiative, he was handing himself over completely into the arms of God. The priest said:

> When the anaesthetist arrived and I had to hand my son over to him, I suddenly knew that I was putting him into God's hands. My responsibility for him, as his earthly father, was at an end. I could let go of my restless, impotent anxieties. In the midst of all the anguish it was like a small inner core of peace.

God does hear. The phoenix rises from the ashes. Death and resurrection are an everyday fact of human experience, as real as pain. The poet Francis Thompson wrote:

> But, when so sad thou canst not sadder
> Cry;—and upon thy so sore loss
> Shall shine the traffic of Jacob's ladder
> Pitched betwixt Heaven and Charing Cross.

So it will be. Amen.

15

PRAYING IN FAILURE

My flesh and my heart may fail: but God is the strength of my heart and my portion for ever.

PSALM 73.26 (RSV)

I want to draw your attention today to a group of people for whom we often forget to pray, or for whom perhaps we half feel we do not want to pray. Yes, we often pray, quite rightly, for the *innocent* victims of injustice, the hostages, those detained in prison without trial. Their undeserved suffering is indeed a heavy burden to bear. But perhaps we do not sufficiently remember those who are *not* innocent, who are not heroes or martyrs of any sort; who are apparently marked for life by a record of failure or sin that cannot be erased. Maybe most of us have not experienced this sense of hopeless failure. But have we not, all of us, had moments, and some of us much longer periods, when we despise ourselves and say 'I'm no good, I'm useless'? We fail, perhaps, in examinations or in business. We are overlooked for promotion or are sacked or made redundant. We never succeed in bettering ourselves financially and end up skimping on a tiny pension. We fail to make friends, we fail in marriage, we fail as parents; we fail to achieve our life's ambition; and if we are Christians we continually fail God and betray him. We are aware of the poverty of our witness to the Gospel, of the inadequacy of our ministry, of the squabbles in our community which we have not managed to heal, and of the lukewarmness of our prayer.

So when we are told that there is no human misery which God, through his divine son, does not know from the inside, we may find ourselves asking if this is really true. For Jesus was not a sinner, nor incompetent, nor found wanting. He was indeed rejected, but it was because of his strength, not because of his weakness. He lived and died triumphantly in God's sight.

Stevie Smith, in a poem called 'Was he married?', expressed this difference with great poignancy:

He was not wrong, he was right,
He suffered from others', not his own, spite.

But there *is* no suffering like having made a mistake
Because of being of an inferior make. . . .

All human beings should have a medal.
A god cannot carry it, he is not able.

Sometimes we can feel that the dice are so loaded against us that we become despairing. And our self-disgust and, often, our anger with God, make it very difficult for us to pray.

1. GOD'S UNFAILING MERCY

(a) Yet it was precisely for people like us that Christ came to earth. Jesus repeatedly stressed that his mission was to the failures, the poor, the outcasts and sinners. What God could never convey to us from the heights of heaven he could show us by coming alongside. And we might reply to Stevie Smith that although we know a great deal about the way Jesus lived, we do not have sufficient data to decide whether or not he knew what it was to feel a failure. What was it really like for him when the rich young ruler turned his back; when he could not get the Jewish leaders to listen to him; when, with only a few weeks of his earthly life remaining, he saw that despite all his teaching his disciples were still naïve enough to be quarrelling about who would be the greatest in the kingdom of heaven? Perhaps the difference between his experience and ours was that he knew absolutely that he must not worry about how other people judged him, or evaluate his life and mission in their terms. How much pain we would be spared if we could once accept that other people's assessment of us is irrelevant, and that we are not even able to judge ourselves, as Jesus showed in his story of the Pharisee and the tax-gatherer. The former had no sense of failure whatever. The tax-gatherer, for his part, felt unable even to lift his eyes to heaven: but it was *his* prayer that was acceptable in God's sight. The fact is that with our limited human perception we are not able to distinguish accurately between 'failure' and 'success'. Mozart mismanaged his life, in some respects, so badly that he died in despairing penury and his body was thrown ignominiously into a paupers' grave. Was he a failure? For all we know, he was thrown straight into the arms of God.

(b) So praying in failure is overwhelmingly a question of trust—trust that whatever our circumstances, and whatever we have done or failed to do, we are not rejected. In my work as a counsellor I see again and again that the turning point in therapy, for sufferers of every kind, comes when they begin to see a faint possibility of allowing themselves to be accepted and forgiven. Archbishop Desmond Tutu has written that 'the worst sin in our society is to have failed. We work ourselves into a frazzle in order to succeed. . . . What a tremendous relief it is to discover that we don't need to prove ourselves to God.' I often think gratefully of the dying thief who was received into the kingdom at the eleventh hour without, apparently, having done anything to deserve it. All he did was ask.

We can ponder, too, the reaction of Simon the Pharisee to the prostitute who anointed the feet of Jesus, his celebrated dinner guest. Simon was so sure that no 'good' or respectable person could allow such a woman to touch him that he assumed Jesus did not perceive the truth about her, and was therefore not a genuine prophet. But of course Jesus knew what Simon was thinking, and challenged him by telling a brief but pointed story about a moneylender who let two men off their debts. One of them owed a large sum, the other much less. 'Now which will love him most?' asked Jesus. Simon was obliged grudgingly to give the only possible answer, 'I should think the one that was let off most'. It is a comment that remains true for all time. The immensity of our failure is matched by the immensity of the love that redeems it, releasing in us the capacity to love in our turn. So we are enabled to pray, against all reason, against all the odds, 'O God, there is no failure so bad that you cannot redeem it; and no sin so great that you cannot forgive it. You are the God who makes all things new.' Such prayer is like a great citadel around us to defend us from despair.

2. OUR RESPONSE

(a) But when we pray in this way we are not asking for a magic wand to be waved, to alter all the inauspicious circumstances of our lives. God will unfailingly accept and support us, but he will not help us to cling to failure, which is what we often try to do. Surrendering our lives to God never means that we can now sit back and vaguely hope that things will be different next time round. The Indian poet Rabindranath Tagore put this beautifully when he wrote of God's 'strong mercy', and of how he saves us by 'hard refusals'. We know in our deepest hearts that when we are in trouble people who offer us glib reassurances are of little use to us: their 'help' evaporates almost before we have closed the door. But God offers us love and truth conjointly, and cannot do anything else, for they are what he is. Our faith in him thus includes the belief that he will use our failure creatively so that we may change and grow, and learn that we are not constrained by destiny to go on sinning or failing again and again in the same old ways. Such a journey can never be without pain for us, but this in itself can be curiously comforting: somehow the hardness of the process gives us confidence in its reality. So we are enabled to accept the pain, and to pray:

> O God, my life is in chaos, but you can bring it into order; I despise myself, but you can help me to let go of my angry despair; I am full of bitterness, but you can teach me how to forgive; I am incompetent, stupid, clumsy, and nervous, but you can give me the serenity I need and the insight to discover my own truth, and to speak it quietly from the heart. I am afraid of others, of the contempt in their eyes and the sharpness of their comment, but you can affirm my inner strength so that I no longer fear that I will be destroyed. You are the strength of my life: of whom then shall I be afraid?

(b) And it is important to remember that all that has been said about failure applies also to our failure in prayer. We may fear that our prayer is totally inadequate, so lacking in faith that it could not possibly be heard. But the glorious truth is that this does not matter. Signals from a space-probe with only the strength of a light bulb can now be picked up and interpreted by people on earth millions of miles away. In the same way God can pick up even the feeblest spark of our faith or contrition or goodwill. Even the briefest signal to him—'Lord, have mercy'—will be heard and amplified a thousand-fold.

So let us go on praying, out of the depths of our weakness and failure, 'Lord, I believe: help thou mine unbelief. My flesh and my heart may fail, but you are the strength of my life, and my portion for ever.'

16

PRAYING IN PROSPERITY

Let not the rich man glory in his riches: but let him who glories glory in this, that he understands and knows me.

JEREMIAH 9.23 (RSV)

One Christmas I was eating a splendid dinner with my youngest sister and her family, when suddenly she put down her knife and fork and said 'Just look at us! Look what we have here! Far more than we need, while there are millions of people starving.' The family began to laugh. This had happened before, and it had become a family joke. 'Ah, here comes Mum's Christmas homily!' Well, perhaps her timing left something to be desired. But I knew it was not really a joke for her: she has many contacts among black Africans and is very conscious of the growing 'underclass' in our own land. I am sure that many of us have shared her sadness and perplexity. While we live so comfortably, do our prayers for the poor and the underprivileged mean anything at all? Our Lord's words seem to leap out at us from the page: 'Go, sell all that you have . . . and come, follow me'.

It seems that we need, to help us in this situation, a 'theology of success'. But I am not sure that this is something that Christians have ever had, though the Victorians, like the Jewish patriarchs, were able to persuade themselves, to some extent, that riches were a direct reward from God for righteous living. Sadly it has long been only too obvious that this happy theory does not accord with the facts. Quite early in the Old Testament we find people daring to say that, on the contrary, it is the ungodly who seem to prosper. And the gospels give us a clear message that the kingdom of heaven belongs not to the rich and powerful but to society's rejects, the poor and the oppressed. Jesus is even on record as having passionately denounced the well-off:

> Woe unto you that are rich for you have received your consolation.
> Woe to you that are full now, for you shall hunger.
> Woe to you that laugh now, for you shall mourn and weep.

And then there is his statement that 'It is easier for a camel to go through the eye of a needle than for a rich man to enter the kingdom of God'.

1. IS IT WICKED TO BE RICH?

(a) So where does that leave most of us, the well-to-do and the comfortable? For by comparison with the Third World or the very poor in our own land, those of us who live even in modest comfort are wealthy indeed. 'They left all and followed him', we are told of the first disciples. So if I know in my heart that in no circumstances could I contemplate doing any such thing, that I depend for my night's sleep on the security of my house, my pension and my savings, how can I sincerely pray each day that others who do not have this security may be comforted?

Of course, there have been men and women down the ages who have been called to take the command literally: monks and nuns who have vowed to renounce all private possessions, people like Mother Teresa who have followed vocations among the poorest of the poor. But common sense tells us that we would not be helping much if we all sold our houses and joined the ranks of the homeless, or cancelled our holidays, thereby depriving thousands in the tourist industry of their livelihood. And if we look more closely at the gospels, we find that in practice Jesus by no means always shunned the well-off. He himself asked to lodge with Zaccheus, a man who was not only rich but had become so through the embezzlement of tax money. Many well-to-do people were numbered among his followers, for instance Joseph of Arimathea, who offered the tomb he had prepared for himself on his private estate, to receive the body of his Lord. So Jesus was buried with dignity in a rich man's garden, and not—as might have seemed to us more in accord with the pattern of his life and death—as an outcast among outcasts in a common grave.

(b) So what was Jesus condemning? Not worldly success in itself, but the harmful effects it may have on human beings, making them arrogant, greedy, corrupt, and callously indifferent to the sufferings of others. It is possible to live in a private, comfortable world without the least understanding of what it is like to be poor and of no account. You will remember the famous remark, supposed to have been made by Queen Marie Antoinette when she was told that the poor had no bread: 'Let them eat cake!' And success can take from us all sense of our own true identity. The author of the Book of Revelation wrote, 'You say, I am rich, I have prospered and need nothing: not knowing that you are wretched, pitiable, poor, blind and naked'. 'So is he', said Jesus, 'who lays up treasure for himself but is not rich towards God.'

2. ACTING OUT OF LOVE

(a) But it does not have to be like this. There is nothing in the world that can prevent us from serving God if that is what, above all, we desire. We do not have to creep before him shamefacedly and full of guilt because we ourselves are not starving. Money can be a snare, or an opportunity for love. So, in prosperity, there can be a great simplicity about our prayer. 'All that I am, Lord, and all that I have and own, is yours.' If we continually pray in this way we can have absolute trust that the discernment for which we ask will be given to us. We may be presented with a very great challenge. But more often what we are shown is simply the next immediate step.

> Keep Thou my feet; I do not ask to see
> The distant scene; one step enough for me.

Christians in every walk of life, just like us, can only safely proceed through a moment by moment dedication to God in the here and now. There is no other way.

(b) So our confidence in how we are living can only arise from this simplicity of surrender. Actions arising from any source other than love—out of guilt, or remorse, or vanity, or even a zeal to do good—never work in the long term, however great our apparent generosity. There is a splendid moment in Jean Anouilh's play *Becket*, where the newly appointed archbishop, determined to take his new position seriously, instantly gives away all the wealth he has accumulated during his years as chancellor of the realm. He is congratulated on this magnificent and apparently saintly gesture. 'Yes', he replies, 'but a true saint would not have given it away all at once!'

'If I give away all I have', wrote St Paul, 'but have not love, I gain nothing.' He might have added that the recipients of my pseudo-generosity will most probably not gain either! Giving without true love—the love that is unconcerned about its own reputation or even its own sinlessness—often places the recipients in a form of bondage instead of setting them free. It has given 'charity' a bad name, with its undertones of patronizing 'do-gooding' that emphasizes the inferiority and weakness of the other and saps initiative and self-respect. True giving is always creative, and there is a mutuality about it. Those who work sincerely with the handicapped or the deprived are typically heard to say, 'They have given me so much'. So we need to pray that we may learn to give, not just because we *have* something to give, but in reverence for those to whom we give it.

(c) So if we keep close to God, our prayer will lead us to the action he has planned for us. But what of the prayer that we offer together? Sometimes our corporate selfishness is very great. Unless our public intercessions, like our private prayer, are prayers of surrender, they can be of no avail. It is so easy for us to slip into an exclusive in-turned 'churchiness' which has little to do with the furtherance of the kingdom of God. So often we put all our energies into keeping our own parish activities going, and have no time to spare for the needs and suffering of those outside our own circle.

> I was hungry, and you discussed my hunger.
> I was naked, and you debated the morality of my appearance.
> I was homeless, and you preached to me of the spiritual shelter of the love of God.
> I was lonely, and you left me alone to pray for me.
> You seem so holy and so close to God—but I am still very hungry, and lonely, and cold.
> ('Listen, Christian'—*Social Justice Newsletter*)

Do we, in our churches, pray sufficiently often and seriously about how we spend, not just our money, but our time? I know a woman who found the demands made on her by her local church so great that she had either to give up her voluntary caring activities in the community or move to another parish. 'Let not the rich man glory in his riches', said Jeremiah. No, not even in the riches of his exclusive salvation. 'Let him who glories glory in this, that he understands and knows me.' To know God is to know love's full meaning—for all mankind. Only by continual prayer can we come to this understanding and knowledge. So let us pray in our prosperity—pray alone and pray together—that we may be given the wisdom to discern and follow the true path of love.

17
THE PRAYER OF OBEDIENCE

Master, we toiled all night and took nothing. But at your word I will let down the nets.

LUKE 5.5 (RSV)

Of all the disciples, Simon is undoubtedly the one to whom the Gospel writers give the most space. His unpredictable and colourful pronouncements made him excellent media material. You could never tell what he would say next—and I think neither could he! He spoke directly out of his feelings in a completely open and spontaneous way. The words here recorded by Luke were spoken when he had just met Jesus for the first time. What a start! Clearly Jesus was moved by his obedience, seeing him instantly as a person of immense potential, someone with whom he could share his life.

One of our most frequent petitions is for the grace of obedience. And there is much in this story to illuminate and reinforce our prayer. For me, one of the most reassuring aspects is that Simon's obedience was a two-stage response. He did not 'hole in one'! At first, he demurred. 'Look, we've already been at it all night!' We can sympathize. When something has not gone right for us we feel we simply cannot summon up the energy and purpose to begin all over again. All the same, we find the idea of instant obedience alluring. We applaud members of the armed forces for obeying without question, and we do not regard this as stupid, but as heroic. However, there are other circumstances in which unquestioning obedience appears in a different light. As parents, we teach our children to obey us, certainly, but we also teach them *not* to obey strangers who tell them to get into the car. And in trials of war criminals, we do not accept 'being under orders' as a valid defence of barbaric acts.

I doubt if God ever expects us to act dumb and forgo all our powers of discernment. Even the most loyal ratings must on occasion have reservations about what they are being told to do. But their training enables them to set these aside by inculcating trust, not for the command, but for the commander. So before we obey an order we need to know from whom it comes. Simon had a chance to assess Jesus because he had just lent him his boat as a temporary pulpit. He had listened to Jesus teaching the crowds. Clearly he had felt the love and goodness and personal authority emanating from this extraordinary man, whom later he was to recognize as divine. We too have to be sure that our orders come from God.

1. RECOGNIZING GOD'S VOICE

(a) How are we to do this? Ultimately, only by walking continually with our Lord in single-minded devotion—like the little dog on the whirling gramophone records of my childish memories, who could recognize His Master's Voice anywhere. But while we are still very much novices, as Simon was on that beach, there are perhaps some pointers we can usefully reflect upon as we pray for grace to obey.

When I was with a group of people training to be counsellors, we were taught—very properly—that before we could hope to be of any use to others we must try to understand something of the complexities of our own natures. We were encouraged to look for and identify what were called our sub-personalities. I gave names to some of mine. There was Melissa, wildly impulsive, and St Joan, who was quite the opposite, impossibly noble and heroic and, I have to say, extremely vain. I began to see that many of the scrapes I had got into during my life had arisen from listening exclusively to one or other of these two. Both of them, like the devil who tempted Jesus, could quote Scripture to great effect. Joan, in particular, was also very clever at imitating God's voice. But gradually I did get better at learning to laugh at these two ladies and to say to them, 'Come off it! A good try, but I know who you are!' Later, I also discovered that God loved them and could use them, as long as they did not try to take over control. So to reflect a little about who we are can help quite a bit in discerning who is giving us orders.

(b) There is something else even more important that we can do, and it may require us to be still in God's presence for quite a long while. We need to look at the command we *think* we are receiving in the light of all that we have glimpsed about God's nature and the nature of his kingdom. Does the proposed action conform with the demands of truth, love, peace, and the other fruits of the Spirit enumerated by St Paul? If after reflection and prayer we feel that the answer is 'yes', or at any rate that it is the nearest we can see, then we must go ahead in faith and trust, knowing that God can use even our errors for good. But if one quality seems to be missing—if we seem to have love without truth, which is sentimentality, or truth without love, which can never actually be the truth—then it is wise to reflect a little longer. This is the stage, too, when it can be an enormous help to test the matter out with a trusted friend or group. God will often show us, through them, what we may have overlooked.

2. OBEYING GOD'S VOICE

So we come to the second stage of the prayer of obedience, the moment of surrender. Cranmer summed it up beautifully when he wrote that God's people should pray 'that they may both perceive and know what things they ought to do, and also may have grace and power faithfully to fulfil the same'. Well, we might think that once we have understood what we are being commanded to do, our difficulties would be at an end. If we truly love God we shall easily and happily comply. Sometimes, of course, we can. But it is not always like that, is it? It may not always be so very difficult to go through the outward motions of obeying. We can often discipline ourselves to do that. But to obey cheerfully, without reservation, with our whole heart—that is a different matter.

Once when I was a junior teacher in the history department of a large school, I was asked by the head of department to look through a list of A-level topics and tell her which I would like to teach the next year. I went through the list of twenty or so topics and gave her my preferences in order, pointing out also the only one I would really dislike. This was the one she finally decided I should do. Obedience was a serious matter in this establishment, and I had to do it. I lacked the confidence to challenge the decision, and I think it would have made little difference if I had. So I was left with strong resentment at the injustice of it. But I knew that my problem was not really that I resented her authority. I knew it was her responsibility to decide what was in the best educational interests of our pupils. No, my problem was that I had been left emotionally and psychologically and, yes, spiritually, so stuck. I needed help—some encouragement, gratitude even—in order that I might find the inner freedom to make my surrender with grace, from the heart. But I was also rather 'hooked' on being noble and not airing grievances. St Joan was in the ascendant! So something that might have been resolved in a few days became for me a prolonged and painful inner labour, despite all my prayer. And my martyred air no doubt poisoned the atmosphere of the whole department the while.

This may seem a rather trivial example. But it makes the point that outward conformity is not enough. The New Testament writers make it clear that the only sacrifice that can possibly forward the kingdom of God is a sacrifice made in love. 'If we give our bodies to be burned, and have not love, we have nothing.' This is not so much a judgement as a statement of observable fact. When we are trapped in bitter resentment we feel cut off from God. We literally have nothing —neither our original desire, nor the joy and peace of acceptance. Sometimes, then, we may need to seek help in discerning what it is in us that is blocking a gracious surrender. This may well be God's will for us if we find that our prayer is not bringing us the healing we desire.

And how infinitely greater the pain is if our obedience entails giving up, not something trivial, but a cherished project, a lifetime's ambition, or, hardest of all, a loved person. Now indeed our determination to pray is put to the test. It is no use dodging the fact that we may have to pray in agony for a while. Perhaps the greatest comfort we can have at such a time is that Our Lord also knew the cost of obedience. If we are praying 'Yet not my will but thine be done', then we can be sure that he is with us in our Gethsemane, sharing our pain. And very gradually we shall find that we begin to have some inner trust that one day healing will come. One day we shall know a blessing far greater than any we could have received without this surrender. One day, again, the light will shine.

18
PRAYING AS WE ARE

And David danced before the Lord with all his might.

2 SAMUEL 6.14 (RSV)

One of the difficulties that we make for ourselves in prayer is in struggling to pray, not as we are, but as we are not! It is curious that we should suppose that God, having made each one of us with a particular temperament, should want or require us to pray as if he had made us differently. However, because we are, most of us, so lacking in confidence and prone to guilt, that is very often how we do feel. We compare ourselves adversely with others whom we suppose to be extremely saintly. Or we may have been taught in childhood by parents or Sunday School teachers that there is a 'proper' way to pray, and the message sinks into us so deeply that in later life we cannot find within ourselves the freedom to grow, experiment and explore. But it is certainly not God's intention that out spiritual energies should be drained away in a desperate struggle to pray in a way that is not natural for us. Prayer then becomes a penance rather than a delight. If we allow ourselves to pray in a way that nourishes us, then we can build up a reserve of spiritual energy which, sooner or later, can be used to explore other less readily available aspects of our own nature and of the nature of God.

1. PRAYER AND TEMPERAMENT

(a) We might perhaps start by asking ourselves a simple question. In order to enjoy the company of someone with whom we are in love, would we be more likely to suggest going to a dance or party or for a quiet walk in the countryside? The odds are that the way we answer this question will have some bearing on the way in which we would most naturally enjoy the company of Our Lord. Lack of understanding of this basic temperamental difference often gives rise to misunderstanding—and, sadly, even contemptuous criticism—among Christian folk. Those who most enjoy praising God with joyful hymns and choruses frequently think of quieter forms of worship as dull and inadequate. On the other hand those who are drawn to more reflective forms of prayer tend to regard the more exuberant worship as superficial and spiritually naïve. For them joy is best expressed deeply within themselves as quiet adoration. But, as Jesus repeatedly emphasized, what matters to God is what is going on in our hearts, our true motivations and desires, not the way in which they are expressed. A clergyman in his diocese once confided to Bishop Edward King his frustration and despair that a country lad when asked, after all his confirmation classes, what he was doing to prepare for communion, replied 'I'se cleaned me boots and put 'em under the bed'! But we are on dangerous ground if ever we try to evaluate the prayers or spiritual activities of others. Think of the parable about the Pharisee and the publican. We might be in for a few surprises!

So if we are one of those—about 75 per cent of the population, so statisticians tell us—whose method of dealing with life is mainly through their senses, we should not hesitate to use these in our approach to God. After all we regard 'coming to our senses' as a test of sanity! The Bible, not surprisingly since it enshrines the message of God to ordinary human beings, is overwhelmingly in tune with this approach. Its spirituality is essentially 'green', firmly set in the midst of the actual environment in which we live. In practical terms this means that we should not be afraid to have colour and life and activity in both our corporate and our private worship—and especially in the latter, since this is likely to be the more difficult of the two for us. Even when we are praying alone we can light a candle, touch or hold a chalice or cross or rosary, focus our eyes on an ikon or picture or on a garden or view beyond our window, if we are lucky enough to have one. We can listen to music, sing a hymn aloud—yes, even in the bath!—or repeat prayers from the liturgy or from compilations made by others. And we can be daring enough to use our bodies to express our prayer. I once watched a group of schoolchildren enacting the scene of the healing of the lepers through physical movement, without words. Their yearning eyes and outstretched arms as they turned towards Jesus showed that they were understanding the story at a far deeper level that if they had stayed in their desks writing about his healing ministry. We are told that David danced before the Lord, and I recently heard of a nun who when she was dying, at the age of eighty-two, revealed that she had often gone into the convent chapel and danced when all her sisters had retired to bed. So if we want to communicate with God through the practical, earthed experiences of our senses, in what might be called 'sacramental living', let us rejoice! We are in good company.

(b) But if we are one of those—statistically fewer—more introverted people who need to have space and stillness in order to survive, and who are drained and exhausted by too much company, noise and talk, then it may be natural for us to worship God in a different way. In public worship such people are drawn to a quiet communion service in the early morning, or to a Quaker meeting, or to a Cathedral evensong where they can be anonymous, where nothing is required of them but to respond silently to the beauty of their surroundings and of the music, to the pervading awesome sense of the presence of God. Whereas the former type would be likely to feel deprived at not being able to join in the singing, criticize the occasion for being 'more like a concert', and complain afterwards to the dean that there should be 'more participation', the contemplative will not have felt in any way excluded, but on the contrary deeply identified with and part of what is going on. In some respects these folk are fortunate. They have no difficulty in praying alone, or in meditating for long periods. It is a delight for them. But the outside twentieth-century world, hyperactive and noisy, caters for them hardly at all, and nor, often, do church services, which are inevitably influenced by the general trend. So it is important that all those who have the responsibility for planning and ordering public worship realize the need to care for and nourish this minority, by providing some 'space' —for instance by having pauses after the reading of the Word, and during the intercessions, and by the inclusion of some hymns in a contemplative mood.

There may be another stumbling block for natural contemplatives. They have probably been brought up to 'say their prayers', and have continued to regard prayer as essentially a matter of talk. As this becomes increasingly burdensome, they may become guilty and afraid. Their prayer is drying up. Of course there may be many reasons for this experience, and careful discernment is always required. But if no other cause presents itself, then they need to be affirmed in their particular vocation to the prayer of silence, and perhaps to receive help in deepening their understanding of it. Often the realization that it is a valid and acceptable form of prayer comes to them as an amazing liberation and release.

2. WHOLENESS IN PRAYER

(a) But, of course, however much we are addicted to solitude, we all need other human beings, and however much we enjoy the company of others, we all need some privacy. In order to be whole, to be fully alive, we need to be aware of the less dominant aspects of our nature, to attend to them and encourage them, and thus to learn to respond to God with our entire being. It is not so much a matter of keeping a balance, which seems to imply that we must stay in the dull middle ground of perpetual compromise, as of being free to explore all aspects of our multi-faceted personalities and of the multi-faceted personality of God. Jesus continually drew attention to this, using the expression 'I am . . .'. 'I am the good shepherd. I am the way. I am the light of the world. I am the bread of life. I am among you as he that serves.' Those around him were able to respond to these different aspects of their Lord, and in so doing they also grew and, as it were, became more than themselves, more than in the past they had been. Peter the impulsive became also Peter the rock. So though in our prayer life it is necessary that we start from where we are—and indeed there is nowhere else that we can truthfully start—over the years we should expect movement and change. The orderly, methodical person may find himself able to shout for joy, and the chorus-of-praise devotee may begin to experience deep satisfaction in meditation. Those who have found liturgical prayer boring may suddenly become aware of its depth and beauty, while those who felt they could never pray in their own words begin to realize that they have more to offer than they ever suspected. And when this happens there is a two-fold blessing. We have both a new experience, and, with it, a realization that there is a sense in which it is not new, but is the uncovering of something which has always been latent within us. We are slowly becoming the true selves whom God already knows and loves.

(b) But not only does our prayer change and develop as the years go by but our moods and attitudes change with the ebb and flow of events day by day, and even, for some of us, hour by hour. Whatever our basic temperamental orientation, we all experience, at some time in our lives, a whole range of emotions—weariness, pain, shock, anxiety, grief, hope and delight. Through all these we can be sustained by having formed a secure and settled habit of prayer. But within this discipline, we should not feel guilty if we pray according to our need. During a difficult time of my life I found that all I could do was to repeat certain verses over and over again endlessly through the day—and sometimes also through the night. 'O send out thy light and thy truth that they may lead me, and bring me to thy holy hill and to thy dwelling.' Or 'The Lord is my shepherd: I shall not want'. Each of us will have our own special life-lines. Sometimes our prayers will pour out of us: sometimes we seem tongue-tied and devoid of inspiration and have to depend on prayers composed by others. 'For everything there is a season, and a time for every matter under heaven', as the author of the book of Ecclesiastes wrote. When the disciples asked 'Lord, teach us to pray' they were not rebuffed, but were given the priceless gift of a prayer surpassing any with which their Jewish heritage had supplied them. And if we, in our turn, ask with equal longing, 'Lord, teach me to pray', we can have the assurance that we will not be sent empty away.

19

DISTRACTIONS IN PRAYER

But the thistles shot up and choked the corn.

MARK 4.7 (NEB)

The other day I heard a woman describe her first experience of a 'quiet day' at a retreat house. She had gone more or less on impulse, feeling a hunger for something she could not define. But she also had considerable misgivings, which her first impressions did nothing to allay. She found herself in the company of a number of women, mostly grey-haired, and very holy. She knew they were holy by their expressions! Most of them appeared to be effortlessly wrapped in deep prayer. Later she began to realize that appearances can be deceptive! Sometimes, it is true, and especially at moments of great distress or solemnity, we are able to pray with intense concentration. We are told that a few moments before Dietrich Bonhoeffer was executed, the prison doctor glimpsed him through the half-open door of one of the huts 'kneeling in fervent prayer to the Lord his God. The devotion and evident conviction of being heard that I saw in the prayer of this captivating man moved me to the depths.' It can move us still, and even reading such a passage can quieten us and provide a powerful antidote to our distractions. But as a rule, in the ordinary routine of our daily lives, we may feel we have more in common with the ridiculous than with the sublime. It is the nursery prayer of Christopher Robin with which we more easily identify:

> God bless Mummy, I know that's right.
> Wasn't it fun in the bath to-night,
> With the cold so cold and the hot so hot—
> Oh, God bless Daddy, I quite forgot!

Our prayers do seem to consist of a series of inconsequential, fleeting moments, a pattern of lapse and recall, of contemplation of our day's schedule or our shopping list mixed up with our contemplation of God. And, whereas we can smile at the innocence of Christopher

Robin and affectionately absolve him, we do not find it so easy to forgive ourselves. We have to admit that sometimes we end our prayer feeling irritable and frustrated rather than refreshed. We know all about the thistles choking the corn.

1. DEALING WITH DISTRACTIONS

(a) It is not difficult to list some of the causes of our distraction. The trouble is that doing so does not make us feel very much better. We know that we cannot really offer them as excuses: We 'ought' to have more self-discipline and a greater desire for God. However it can be a worthwhile practice to stop the drift occasionally and examine what is going on in our own individual lives. To know more precisely what is disturbing us may make it easier to find an appropriate solution.

A first difficulty may be the external one of noise and lack of privacy. When we live in small houses, perhaps with a boisterous young family, and do not have a bedroom to ourselves, then, however considerate our spouse, this can be a real problem. It may be possible for us to get up earlier and pray while the house is quiet, or to find a space during the day when the children are at school, or, if we go to work, to spend a few moments in a nearby church in our lunch hour. But the important thing is to realize that it is not so much the noise and bustle in themselves that impede us, as our reaction to them. It is possible to learn to isolate ourselves temporarily and create our own inner space and peace. I saw a good example of this once when I was given the task of helping some fifty 'beginners' to explore the prayer of silence. When we arrived at the hall where the session was to take place, we discovered that the local Cubs were having their annual party in the adjacent room. So there were continual joyful sounds, whoops and shrieks, stamping feet and banging of doors. The noise was so deafening that we had virtually to communicate by sign language.

What were we to do? We could perhaps have searched out the verger and asked him to re-open a nearby church which had been closed for the night. But there was a more valuable lesson to be learned by staying where we were. So we began by focusing our full attention on these small boys, asking for God's blessing on the party and on each individual child. Then, when it was time to turn to our own appointed task, we decided to let go of these sounds. We gathered them up and gently, without struggle, put them aside—almost with a physical gesture. A great hush fell among us in our room. It was as if we were in a cocoon of peace. It was one of the most deeply quiet moments I have ever experienced, and afterwards I discovered that the others who were present had felt the same. God was truly in our midst. Perhaps it is easier to practise 'peace-making' in this way when we have the support of others, but it can be done alone—on a railway station, in a supermarket, anywhere. To pray in this way, continually throughout the day, can become a marvellous hallowing of the whole of our lives.

(b) The secret of this method of dealing with distractions is, of course, the absence of struggle, and we can often defuse our inner worries in a similar way, by first giving them our total concentration, offering them to God, and then gently setting them aside. For as soon as we fight something, inside or out, most of us at once experience tensions that are counterproductive. But there are indeed some people who are able to tackle distractions head-on, by sheer self-discipline. Simone Weil, a young French philosopher and passionate campaigner for social justice, wrote about her method of praying the Lord's Prayer:

> I have made a practice of saying it through once each morning with absolute attention. If during the recitation my attention wanders or goes to sleep, in the minutest degree, I begin again until I have once succeeded in going through it with absolutely pure attention. . . . The effect of this practice is extraordinary and surprises me every time, for although I experience it every day, it exceeds my expectation at each repetition.

We must not ignore the possibility that this might be a way forward for some of us, too.

(c) But if our preoccupations or trivial wanderings obstinately refuse to be banished on any particular occasion, then it may be that we are to regard them, not as distractions, but as the necessary substance of our prayer. If I am struggling to pray with concentration for a sick neighbour, or to give thanks for some happy event, and my mind constantly diverts itself instead to a conversation or letter that has left me feeling uneasy or upset, then it may be that, at this moment, my neighbour and my gratitude are the distractions, and it is the disturbing conversation that I should be bringing before God. God meets us always where we actually are, not where we are not, nor where we think we ought to be. So we have to be prepared to recognize that our wandering may not be 'failure', but the direct guidance of the Holy Spirit. In that case we will have no peace until we surrender. I once heard a monk say that he never had any distractions, because he always prayed right away about anything that entered his head! We may be truly closer to God if we simply let our prayers flow with the currents of our lives.

2. TURNING TO GOD

For although it is necessary and valuable, for truth's sake, occasionally to think about the feebleness of our prayer, and to explore ways in which it might be deepened—as we are now doing—there is danger in this approach if it is carried to excess. It keeps our attention still primarily focused on ourselves. But prayer is not a matter of self-improvement. Its essence is a turning outward to God, allowing him to draw us to himself like a magnet we cannot resist. Our restless minds can be so captivated by God, so absorbed in him, that we simply lose awareness of our self-centred concerns.

Recently on a dark December morning I woke early and switched on my bedside lamp. The window curtains were drawn back, but all I could see outside was the blackness of the sky, and my own lamp, now mysteriously removed into a flowerbed like a flying saucer in miniature. But when I switched it off, all was changed. There was the shadowy outline of a hill, and the graceful shapes of leafless trees standing together in the silver-grey light of early dawn. All around was the mysterious hint of a greater light yet to come. It was magically beautiful. Yet, blinded by my own lamp, I might never have known it was there.

So if we turn from the artificial light of our own knowledge and effort to contemplate the poetry and beauty and mystery that lie beyond, we shall not have to worry about distractions. They will simply be eclipsed. More than that, when we take up our daily lives again we often find that, while we have been with God, they have actually been dissipated and healed. So let us pray with St Paul that our thoughts may be filled with all that is true, all that is just and pure, all that is lovely and full of grace, all that is excellent and worthy of praise. And may the God of peace be with us all.

20

PRAYER IN A BUSY LIFE

'Could you not watch with me one hour?'

MATTHEW 26.40 (RSV)

These words, of course, were spoken by Jesus in very special and poignant circumstances. The three disciples whom he had taken with him when he prayed in Gethsemane had fallen asleep. They were not fully aware of his agony, or of his need of them. They had not been able to remain alert even in the face of obvious danger. They had not even realized how stern a test they themselves were about to face, nor their need to prepare for it. That night they were to learn a heart-rending lesson about the necessity of prayer. After that night, as the book of the Acts of the Apostles makes clear, they depended on it absolutely. Prayer became the mainstay of their lives.

Is it like that for us? Most of us would have to admit that it is not. Often we pray with urgency at times of great sorrow or anxiety. But in our day-to-day lives, I wonder what we would have to reply if Jesus were to address a similar question to us? Often we would feel like saying 'Lord, you know I can't. An hour? You must be joking! I can hardly spare five minutes.' I suppose there *are* people who are conscious of having a great deal of uninterrupted leisure, long silent hours when they can be still with God. But I do not seem to meet them! We are all rushing about, and the air must be full of the sharp arrow prayers we send up in transit.

1. BEING TOO BUSY

Of course I am not decrying these brief minute-by-minute contacts. They are a vital part of our walk with God, and in times of emergency they can sustain us for weeks. But to sustain us for life something more is needed. For really nourishing prayer, out of which change and growth can come, we have to find time to be still and reflective in God's presence. Being with God in this way is the very essence of prayer. So what prevents us from doing this? I daresay you have found, as I have, that when people discuss the difficulties they have with prayer, the same few themes recur again and again: I can't find the time; I am too tired; I am too easily distracted; I lack the discipline. And of these, 'being busy' seems to have a clear lead.

Perhaps we should examine this notion that 'being busy' is a chief obstacle to prayer. The implication is that it would be easier to pray if we were *not* busy. But I have a suspicion that we may be deluding ourselves, and that people who do not pray when they are busy do not pray when they have leisure either! Perhaps there is no dodging the fact that whether we pray or not depends largely on the importance we attach to it. If we hunger and thirst to be with God we shall somehow find time to pray, as the apostles did. Gandhi used to say that he could go without food—and we know this was no idle boast—but he could not do without God for a single minute. But, you may say, if we are going to be realistic, most of us are not like that. Lord, you know that I love you. But my love is not yet enough.

So what holds us back? A long day at the office, a family with three children coming to stay, redecorating the kitchen, getting up early to make Bill's sandwiches, preparing for the committee meeting or the Bible Study group. You know how it goes. Yet I want to suggest that the real problem may not lie so much in our busyness as in our attitude to it.

2. BEING UNDER STRESS

(a) Once on a visit 'down under' I was standing on a traffic island in the middle of a busy Sydney street. Suddenly, out of the traffic, an exceptionally tall man, wearing, as I recall, a green jacket, appeared at my side. It was obvious that he had been refreshing himself fairly thoroughly during his lunch break. In what I took to be an East European accent he asked a single question: 'What is destroying the West?' Despite the unusual circumstances I felt that this was a serious question deserving a serious answer. But there was no time to think, and the word that I heard coming out of my mouth was 'stress'.

He nodded, and sighed, and then the sign flashed 'walk' and I watched him drift away through the crowds. But I think about him still.

Afterwards I wished I had said, 'We are out of touch with God; we do not pray', because there is a link between stress and not praying. Although we blame 'being too busy' for our failure to pray, often the real culprit is our underlying stress, our tensions and uncertainties. Subconsciously we often choose to be too busy, using it as a drug to blot out the malaise we do not wish to perceive. Perhaps we are not always as anxious for God to speak to us as we think we are! It may be safer not to give him the chance.

(b) There is another way in which stress can lead to our being too busy. We are often too 'wound up' to be able to discern the shortest and simplest way to carry out our tasks. 'Forgive this long letter: I haven't time to write a short one'! It may also take us too long to make relatively simple decisions. For Emily, aged four, Christmas Day was too long and too exciting. When bedtime approached, and her mother asked her what she would like for her supper, she burst into tears and said 'I've lost my think'. We all know how that feels! But it does not always occur to us that we might find our 'think' again quite quickly if we were to have even a few minutes of quiet with Our Lord, to put things into perspective. Prayer is a great time-saver, if we will allow it to be so.

Because of all these underlying aspects of our busyness, it becomes very important for us, too, to look at our bulging diaries with a critical eye. Often there does not appear to be a single thing that we can weed out. Everything seems to be a duty laid upon us by God. But if we look again, can we really find nothing, nothing at all, that we are doing out of vanity, because we were flattered to be asked? Or through our distrust of the competence of others, or our obsessive desire for tidiness and efficiency? Or because of our need to be needed, or liked, or thought good? We ought perhaps to be more suspicious of our busyness. The older I grow, the more I come to feel that overwork may not be a virtue. On the contrary, it may be a serious sin, coming between us and God.

3. LIFE AS PRAYER

But, of course, there are some for whom busyness is inescapable. I think of Jane, a young mother coping with triplets, now aged twenty months, and a daughter aged four. She has forgotten what it is like to have any continuous sleep, or even to sit down. Yet she goes about her impossible twenty-hour shifts with astonishing love and serenity. Her whole life seems to be a prayer. So thinking of her, and others like her, brings me back to what I said earlier, that it is not our busyness that keeps us from God so much as our attitude to it.

George Herbert saw this very clearly when he wrote the poem which we use as a hymn, about sweeping a room 'as for thy laws'. Using the vacuum cleaner or the lawnmower may be a rushed, irritating interlude through which our inner tension is increased. But if we have a deliberate consciousness of sharing the whole of our lives with God, then we can perform such tasks with serenity: our awareness of his presence makes such moments part of our prayer. In his book called *Holiness*, Donald Nicholl writes of a monk who said to a visitor 'You must learn how to eat an orange'. 'But I've just eaten one.' 'But I don't think you have! You were concentrating on preparing the second segment whilst you were eating the first. You have finished the orange without really eating it at all.' This kind of hurry, says Donald Nicholl, is a form of greed. It is the opposite of holiness. Perhaps we need to look again, in this activist age, at what we mean by living a holy life.

So when we pray 'Take from our lives the strain and stress', we are not just asking God to give us more time, though, as we have seen, that is something he may be longing to do. We are also asking for our attitude to our daily life to be transformed. And if this happens, even to a small degree, then mysteriously we find that we do actually have more time, and more space, and more inclination to pray. It may even be that if Our Lord should ask us 'Could you watch with me one hour?', we should be able to reply, with joy, 'Yes, Lord, I believe I can'.

21

PRAYING WITH OUR WHOLE SELVES

Here we offer and present unto thee, O Lord, ourselves, our souls and bodies.

(BCP)

As a child being brought up in a rectory I was, of course, taken regularly to church on Sundays, with my three sisters. I remember being excruciatingly bored, as the voices droned on interminably through Matins and the pew became harder and harder. Sunday School in the afternoons was even worse. The only alleviating factor was that I might be able to please teacher by answering all the questions correctly. It is obvious looking back that I was a horrible, smug little girl. But, despite this, God in his mercy must have intended my salvation, for, once a month, I was given something so beautiful that I needed no persuasion of its importance. This was the Sung Eucharist, which, paradoxically, was the only service I had to beg to go to, because I 'would not understand'. Of course it is true that I did not understand, in any intellectual sense. But the whole effect of it, the music, the candles, the words so solemnly and reverently spoken and, above all, the pervading sense of mystery and awe, conveyed the certainty that here was something infinitely precious, for which I longed. So it was in this situation, so utterly 'beyond' me, so incomprehensible in human terms, that I first became aware of the existence of another dimension, which later I would learn to call divine.

It would be easy to explain this away by saying that I fell in love with beauty, not with God. And, of course, I had yet to learn that this new dimension could not be used as a way of escape from life; that it embraced not only beauty but also human ugliness, suffering and despair. Nevertheless, I did absorb from this experience an important truth—that God cannot be known through reason and intelligence alone, but that he speaks to us in our whole being, and calls to our whole being to respond.

1. THE ALIENATION OF OUR PHYSICAL SELVES FROM GOD

Yet, as Jung in our time has so forcefully pointed out, in our Western culture we have become so alienated from our instinctual roots that we tend to be deeply suspicious of our senses, our feelings, our dreams and intuitions. We regard reason and logic as being the only safe guides for our lives. Yet in common speech we talk of 'coming to our senses' as a test of sanity! In his book *The Human Cycle* the anthropologist Colin Turnbull has written of the striking difference in the way in which 'physical development' is regarded in a typical English public school and among the Mbuti tribe of north-east Zaire. In his own youth, it meant the number of inches he grew and 'brute strength in sport'. But among the Mbuti it means 'exploring and developing to the limit all their powers and senses—sight, smell, touch, hearing—all nurtured as instruments of learning and communication'. How much of this wisdom we have forgotten, although the Bible is full of it. We are paying a heavy price for our 'civilization'. It has largely cut us off from the deep wells of our existence, that level where, above all, we can meet with God.

But it does not have to be so, and indeed with the rapid growth of environmental awareness and of holistic approaches in psychology and medicine, it seems that we may have perceived just in time the danger that we have been bringing upon ourselves. Are we on the road back to true sanity and to God? We can now, perhaps, offer in prayer the closing words of the Prayer Book Communion Service with a greater understanding than has been possible for many decades. 'Here we offer and present unto you, O Lord, our selves, our souls and bodies.' We know that it is our whole selves, not just our 'souls', that we are offering to God.

2. SOME WAYS OF PRAYING

(a) How can we translate such an understanding into the actual practice of our prayer? In the first place we can allow ourselves to make full use of all our faculties and senses without embarrassment, and without the half-guilty assumption that somehow we 'ought' to be able to manage without having recourse to them. We can simply accept that what our bodies do affects our minds, and especially our concentration in prayer.

I once lived in Egypt in a suburban flat at the edge of the desert, from which I watched, day by day, workers on a building site close by. It was impossible not to be moved by the instant cessation of work at the call of the muezzin, and the sight of rows of bodies prostrated in reverence on the dusty ground. But many of us have never known, not even in despair, how it feels literally to throw ourselves at Christ's feet, as Jairus did. And it is quite rare now for us to kneel when we pray alone, even for a brief moment, or to bow our heads, or fold our hands in that lovely gesture of supplication and surrender which Mary makes in so many classical pictures of the Annunciation. Anyone who has ever watched, or better still taken part in, a religious dance group will know what a profound effect such movement and gesture can have on us. So if ever we feel able to allow our bodies to participate in our prayer, we should not hesitate to do so. We are praying to the God whose Son took bread and broke it, and made this simple physical gesture into the most powerful symbolic action of all time.

(b) We can make use of our individual senses, too—our sight and hearing and touch. We can listen to Bach or Mozart or to music from Taizé; or watch a candle flame or a sunset; or hold a chalice or pebble or leaf; or gaze at a cross or ikon or into a starlit sky. If any of these are the quickest, simplest way of putting us in touch with our inner selves, then they are also the quickest, simplest way of preparing ourselves for communion with God. It is strange how tenaciously we cling to our belief that prayer ought to feel like a penance, so that the idea of making it easier for ourselves seems almost wicked! But Jesus urged his hearers to set aside their adult inhibitions and approach God with simple directness. He wanted prayer to be the most natural thing in the world for us.

But why is it that the contemplation of material objects—earth, fire, water, wine or bread—can give us such peace? In part it is because they often have a significance greater that their outward forms. They are symbols, which positively help us to identify God's presence in our daily lives. One of the meanings of the Greek word *symbolon* is a token or ticket, a means of identification. Often symbols were two halves of a broken object, that could be fitted back together.

One person had a half, which could be produced to match the other half held by someone else. We can still trace an echo of this idea in the simple ritual of having our tickets torn in half as we enter a theatre or cinema. The two halves are 'symbols', conveying the message that our presence is accepted and approved. So, in the sacrament of the Mass, we on earth have the bread, and Christ has the meaning: the two halves are brought together to make a most glorious whole. And we can think of the woman of Samaria who drew water from the well and offered it to Jesus at his request. In that hot, barren country water was already a precious necessity of bodily life. But Jesus endowed it with completely new meaning. For this woman, 'water' was transformed. That well would never again be 'just a well' for her. Ever afterwards she would draw water, as we eat bread, in remembrance of him.

(c) However, for some of us, it will always be words rather then objects that are of most help in stilling us and directing our thoughts towards God. But words, too, can affect us on different levels. We often think that their sole purpose is to convey precise meanings, but the Bible abounds in the sort of poetry that touches us not only with its sense but through its rhythm and cadence and sheer beauty, much as music does. Think of some of the verses in the book of Isaiah, or Revelation, or the Psalms. 'Arise, shine, for thy light is come.' 'And the desert shall rejoice, and blossom as the rose. . . . And a highway shall be there and a way; and it shall be called the way of holiness.' 'For with you is the well of life: and in your light shall we see light.' 'The Lord is my shepherd: I shall not want. . . . Yea, though I walk through the valley of the shadow of death, I will fear no evil, for thou art with me. . . .'

It is good for all of us to compile our own anthologies of passages that particularly speak to us, and even to memorize as many as we can. They are a resource for life, even in pain—perhaps especially then.

CONCLUSION

So we can long to live in wholeness or 'holiness' by surrendering our whole selves to God, including our bodily faculties and senses. 'O Lord, with my body I honour you: all that I am I give to you.' Let there not be a single cell within me, Lord, from which you are barred, or in which you are denied. My heart and my flesh rejoice in the living God.

22

PRIVATE AND CORPORATE PRAYER

I will bless the Lord at all times: his praise shall continually be in my mouth.

PSALM 34.1 (AV)

A Quaker friend of mine was asked recently why she bothered to do a fifteen-mile journey to the nearest Meeting House on a Sunday morning, there to sit in silence for an hour with a group of people, and return home. What was the point of it? Could she not do whatever she did just as well by sitting in her own home? She replied that it was 'a cherished experience', and that she felt a deep sense of communion with her fellow worshippers as she and they together 'opened their minds and hearts to the ascendancy of God'. We know how she felt. From time to time—or perhaps very frequently—we are made aware in our congregations of an intensity of worship greater than the sum of the contributions made by the individual worshippers. God is with *us* in a very special way, not necessarily more beautiful, but subtly different from the way in which he is with *me.*

A solitary Carmelite monk, however, was once asked the opposite question, 'How do you manage so continually to pray alone? Is it not a lonely and difficult exercise?' His reply was that the situation did not arise. He never did pray alone. Always his prayer was 'with' others. His physical isolation in no way separated him from his fellow human beings and from the realities of the suffering world. We have similar testimony from many who have not chosen to be alone but have been compelled by circumstances so to be. Gonville ffrench-Beytagh has written of his time of imprisonment in Johannesburg, for his opposition to apartheid. 'Although I was in solitary confinement', he said, 'I never had such a sense of belonging in all my life.' In his prayer he was given, to sustain him, 'the sense of being with the company of Christ's beloved'.

So, although the questions were different, it turns out that the answers were very much alike. Both these people—one in company, one alone—had a sense of communion with God and of communion with their fellows. It seems that private and corporate prayer may not be as sharply contrasted as we sometimes think!

1. PRAYING ALONE

(a) But of course none of us is capable of holding our awareness of 'self' and 'other' in perfect balance all the time. There are times in our lives when we need more solitary prayer than shared prayer, and times when it is the other way round. In intense personal need 'Help *me*, Lord', not 'help *us*' may be all we can say. We long for anonymity and privacy—to pray alone, or to worship in a church where no one will require of us even a cheerful 'Good morning'. One of the important services rendered by our cathedrals is surely just this, that they are places into which people can gravitate with their sorrows, knowing that they will be free from questioning voices and prying eyes. A woman who had sought such a refuge, like Hannah weeping in the Temple, wrote afterwards of the 'sudden, unexpected moment of resurrection' that the sheer beauty of the place had given her, even though it was only a brief glimpse of hope:

> God does not even wait
> for me to say thank-you. He is gone
> before the sunset pink can fade
> from the flushed stones, yet leaving
> enough of certainty for me to live on
> for quite a long while, even, perhaps,
> a twelve-month, if I must.

(b) But even in our ordinary routine lives, the difficulty of ever having enough 'aloneness' is for many one of the chief obstacles to private prayer. Jesus knew all about this human need to be alone. Frequently we are told that he withdrew 'to a lonely place apart'. After the feeding of the five thousand he sent the disciples off in the boat, dismissed the crowds, and 'went up on the mountain by himself to pray'. A thousand years before, the poets and musicians at the court of King David had explored the whole range of solitary prayer in their songs, with a beauty never since surpassed. In these verses it seems that all the thoughts and emotions of the human mind and heart are expressed and offered to God. There are prayers made in joy and thankfulness, in humility and longing, in anxiety and fear, in penitence and contrition, in contentment and love and ecstatic delight. The relationship of the praying individual with God is close and intimate. 'O Lord, thou hast searched me out and known me: thou knowest my down-sitting and my uprising; thou understandest my thoughts long before. . . . For lo, there is not a word in my tongue: but thou, Lord, knowest it altogether.' 'Thou art a place to hide me in.' 'Into thy hands I commend my spirit.' 'All my fresh springs are in thee.'

(c) However, despite this mystical inheritance, it seems that the disciples were at first quite bewildered by the intense, solitary, devotional prayer practised by Jesus. They felt at a loss. Luke even refers to an occasion when Jesus was '*praying alone in the presence of his disciples*'! Later, on a similar occasion, they waited until he had finished, and then one of them asked 'Lord, teach us to pray'. Why was it puzzling for them? Partly, no doubt, because the Jewish tradition had always emphasized above all the prayer of the worshipping community. There was a strong sense among ordinary folk that prayer was more likely to be heard if it was offered by the congregation or, better still perhaps, by some especially holy person on their behalf. In Jesus' day, only the High Priest could enter the Holy of Holies, and that only once a year on the Day of Atonement, to intercede on behalf of the people and ask forgiveness for their sin. Private prayer was less stressed, though it was of course practised—not always very privately! You remember that Jesus rebuked the Pharisees for their ostentatious personal devotions, uttered aloud at street corners. Instead, he taught, 'Go into your room and shut the door, and pray to your Father who is in secret; and your Father who sees in secret will reward you'—that is, he will give to each one of you his mercy and blessing in full measure. No intermediary is required. Even sinners can come into God's presence. When we reflect on these historical perspectives we can see even more clearly how astonishing was the teaching of Jesus about the relationship between God and man. Can it really be so close? It is above all through our private prayer that this assurance comes to us.

2. PRAYING IN THE CONGREGATION

(a) Yet when Jesus responded to that request, 'Lord, teach us to pray', the prayer that he gave to his disciples—and to us—was essentially a group prayer. '*Our* Father . . . give *us* this day . . . as *we* forgive.' One night when I was following a television series about the development of the English language, someone began to speak this prayer in the Saxon tongue of our early ancestors. It was a riveting moment. Suddenly I realized that the hills around our village had heard this very sound centuries before. Some unknown man or woman had offered this same prayer, perhaps standing on the very piece of earth where my house is built. I felt that I understood as never before what it means to say 'Thine is the kingdom, for ever and ever'.

It is, of course, partly from this sense of timelessness that our corporate prayer derives its special quality. Individuals come and go, but the prayer of the community of faith never ceases. In our ancient churches it is as if the prayer had soaked into the very stones, and in modern buildings too it is surprising how quickly deep peace takes possession. Of course we can worship anywhere: buildings are only buildings. Solomon had no false sentimental illusions about the Temple which it had been his life's work to build. 'But will God indeed dwell with man on this earth? Behold, heaven and the highest heaven cannot contain thee; how much less this house that I have built.' But, all the same, he knew it was very precious. We do not need to despise ourselves because beauty speaks to us of God. We simply need to retain our awareness that our corporate prayer absolutely transcends the surroundings in which it is offered. Recently I heard a former army officer, now a priest, describe a Communion service shared with a group of men recently captured by the Germans, during the long, exhausting march to Colditz. It was celebrated in a barn with a raw potato, discovered under some straw, and a tin mug of cold water. It was one of the most moving experiences of his life.

(b) And it is worth reflecting on the title of the Prayer Book which has nourished the Anglican Church for three centuries—the Book of Common Prayer. This of course does not mean ordinary and unimportant prayer, but the prayer that we offer together. Within it, in one of Cranmer's collects, we read that we are those 'to whom

Thou hast given a hearty desire to pray'. The 'we' is the praying community. Even if we ourselves hardly pray at all, we are part of this community of faith. Even if we imagine that we are praying alone, it is not so. God is never 'mine'; he is for all mankind. The 'hearty desire to pray' may fluctuate in our churches, but, as Neville Ward has said, it is 'never completely lost, again and again burning up, like a fire whose withered ashes deceive you into thinking it is out, and in our time a flame of increasing power'.

So our common prayer is not just a ritual performed by members of a religious club. And we do not come together solely to make a joyful noise unto the Lord, nor so that we can offer him petitions with many signatures, nor even simply to celebrate the Eucharist. 'You are the light of the world', said Jesus. *Are* we? As C. S. Lewis pointed our, when we look around the pews, we simply see our neighbours 'who sing out of tune, or have boots that squeak, or double chins'. We know we are all faintly ridiculous. So it is hard for us to take Christ's words seriously: and those who do truly consider themselves the light of the world do not always commend themselves to us for their humility and sensitivity! But there it is. 'You are the light of the world. Let your light so shine before men.' Our worshipping communities are like Olympic runners carrying the light of God on their limited sector of the human journey through time and space, and then handing it over to others. The light shines in darkness, and the darkness has not overcome it. In twenty centuries, it has not done so. And it never will.

23

PRAYING IN GROUPS

For where two or three are gathered in my name, there am I in the midst of them.

MATTHEW 18.20 (RSV)

One of the greatest signs of vitality in all the Christian churches at present must surely be the burgeoning of small groups engaged in a great variety of religious activities—Bible Study groups, prayer groups, groups involved with the ministry of healing and so on. But of course group prayer is not a modern phenomenon. For at least the first two centuries of the Christian era it was by far the most common way of praying. The Jews had always believed that the appropriate forum for prayer was, above all, the worshipping community. Their religious life centred on the synagogue and the regular rituals of family worship with occasional visits to the Temple as prescribed in the Law. But for the first Christians there was little possibility of full congregational worship, because converts from Judaism were no longer accepted in synagogues, and the numbers of Gentile Christians in any given locality were still small. Often, too, there was a need for secrecy in times of persecution. So they met in each other's houses, or sometimes out of doors. We know that in the weeks following Our Lord's death, the disciples, in great need of each other's support and fellowship, prayed together continually, and were joined by members of Jesus' own human family, his mother and brothers. Group prayer is referred to throughout the book of the Acts of the Apostles and in St Paul's letters. It was the norm. And we can be sure that our group prayer will be equally hallowed and blessed.

1. THE USES OF GROUP PRAYER

(a) But, of course, our situation is very different. There are plenty of opportunities for congregational worship in church, chapel or

Meeting House. So whether or not we should experience regular prayer in a smaller group is a matter of individual choice. Certainly God may not be calling us to pray in this way. We may, rightly, feel that there is no great gap in our prayer life and that our diaries would be wrongly overloaded. But we may also feel rather suspicious of, or even patronizing towards, those who do join such groups. Are they in some way spiritually deficient so that they are not able to communicate with God on their own? Or are they spiritual snobs, needing to see themselves as an exclusive club with special gifts? It is as well for us occasionally to ask ourselves a few honest questions! Is it by any chance not those others, but I myself, who am the snob? Do I want to keep my God to myself and not share him with others—to privatize my piety? Or do I fear that I might have to allow others to come closer to me, when I would rather keep them at a distance? Or that I am unworthy, not sufficiently 'holy'?

A woman recently said to me that when she joined a prayer group she was asked why, and did not dare to say that it was because she was desperate to find some way of 'getting out of the house', and away from the pressure of her loneliness and other accumulated troubles. Fortunately, the group did respond sensitively to her, and after a while she began to feel there was truly a niche for her there. Groups can be a marvellous source of fellowship, support and encouragement for their members, and a forum for learning and growth. They can also provide a discipline and regularity to see us through times of weariness or inertia. For most people, praying together becomes an enrichment to which they look forward each week.

(b) But, of course, the prime purpose of such a group is not to serve its members, valuable though that is, but to enable them the better to serve God. This is the common purpose which draws them together and from which their deep fellowship grows. And many forms of prayer take on a new dimension when practised in groups. Here we can find the time and space, for instance, to pray for others with a depth and seriousness that is not easily achieved within the more formal constraints of liturgical worship. In our small, intimate circle we have a very special opportunity for holding individuals and specific difficulties quietly before God. We can allow ourselves to be used as channels of his redemptive love, which is the very essence of intercessory prayer.

Groups are also splendid forums for meditation and the prayer of silence. People often say that they cannot meditate because they 'don't know enough' or 'have no imagination'. But in a group which, for instance, studies a Bible passage and then uses it as material for prayer, many will feel able to contribute their own personal insights, and it becomes an enrichment for all. However, it may seem strange to suggest that *silent* prayer may be easier in a group. We associate silence with being alone, and imagine that we will be embarrassed at sitting silently with others. Once when I was a retreat house warden, a visiting priest told me that he thought silent retreats were an affront to God: he made human beings to communicate! But do we communicate only with words? When people are in love their deepest communication is in silence. Words can be barriers between us, and it is an accepted convention that we should use them in this way. If someone asks you how you are, would you be more likely to reply 'I'm fine, thank you', or 'I think my heart is broken'? But in silence, without any prying, curiosity or obtrusiveness, we become more deeply aware of the truth of each other, at the same time that we become more aware of the truth of God, and of his infinite compassion, mercy and love. The two processes are woven together. So 'communication' is transformed into 'communion'. A Quaker friend of mine describes it as her 'most cherished experience'. Often at such a time we are given a profound sense of the presence of God in our midst, something to carry away with us into the hustle of our daily lives.

2. SOME POSSIBLE PITFALLS

(a) But these rich possibilities are not always explored. Because, quite naturally, people of similar outlook and temperament are drawn together, there is a tendency to use one way of praying and one only—praise, for instance—perhaps for years on end. This is not to underestimate for one moment the importance of praise. But what we give can sometimes hide what we withhold, and we may use a superficial joy to avoid facing real difficulties. Another sign that a group is becoming inturned and restricted in outlook is that a sort of jargon develops. When extempore prayer is offered within the same closed group, both the content and the language tend to become narrower and narrower, until, ultimately, very few concepts or ideas are being used. Yet another 'narrowing' that may occur is in our picture of God. Unwittingly we scale him down to fit our limited human perceptions, and see him only as a 'Father in heaven', or as 'Jesus, friend and brother', God made man. Or we concentrate all our thought on the Holy Spirit, and on the way he empowers us to act in the world. Then there is a real danger that we may begin to think of ourselves as infallible, and forget that we are, and always will be, also weak and misguided, continually in need of protection and forgiveness. The symbolism of the Trinity is not just an accident. It corresponds to a vital reality in the wholeness of our perception of God and of ourselves. We too are a trinity of mind, body and spirit. So the three-fold vision brings our fragmented life into a unity.

(b) How are we to guard against such aberrations? Perhaps mainly in three ways. First, by making sure that we are ready to welcome new members into the group from time to time, and also to let people go without recrimination. Second, by sometimes using prayers written by others, which are available to us in the liturgy and in many precious anthologies. And third, by reminding ourselves continually that we are branches of a far larger tree. However close our group is to God, it is composed of human beings; and as human beings our propensity for 'following the devices and desires of our own hearts' is infinite. It is mere arrogance to suppose that we can ever safely and completely 'go it alone'. God can never be our private possession. Our spirituality is personal, yes, but it is also universal. There is abundant evidence of how 'cultic' groups can become if they perceive themselves as separated from others. We have to cherish our own individuality and at the same time our willingness to listen. So all groups need to look at themselves from time to time to ensure that all is well.

CONCLUSION

But if all prayer is an adventure, praying in groups is perhaps especially so. The influence of such prayer in the community within which it is offered is incalculable. Often whole churches seem to come alive after the establishment of one such cell. And when we pray in this way, we are the heirs and companions of countless small groups who, over the centuries, have come together in danger, in persecution, in hope and prosperity; in ancient Rome and in twentieth-century Auschwitz; in monastic cells and inner-city halls; in tropical villages and suburban living-rooms. And for all of them, down the ages, Christ has honoured his promise, as he will do for us. He is truly there in our midst.

24
PRAYER IN COMMITTEE

Except the Lord build the house, they labour in vain that build it.

PSALM 127.1 (AV)

When we meet together as Christian congregations for worship we do not as a rule expect that the preacher will be heckled or that bickering will break out among us. Certainly, in the history of the churches, there have been occasions when this has happened. John Wesley and the Tractarians were no strangers to violent disruption. But usually we are aware that we have met for the purpose of worshipping God and we would regard such interruptions as unseemly and irreverent. However, it is not always quite the same at the meetings of the Parochial Church Council or the General Synod! At these and similar business meetings of the church our immediate purpose is not to worship God but to consider how best to serve him. We have gathered with the intention of discussing and making decisions, and disagreements are inevitable. We realize, of course, that we are still in God's presence and that we are, if anything, even more in need of his help and guidance when we try to put our Christian aspirations into practice. We make a serious effort to remind ourselves of this by starting our meetings with prayer. We may have a moment of silence. Then we snap into business mode and begin to tackle the agenda. We have now, rightly, to concentrate on the matter in hand. Probably we do not directly approach or confer with God again until the end, when we ask for his blessing on our decisions.

What happens in the middle of this 'sandwich' of prayer? If a stranger were to slip in unnoticed and listen to our discussions he would, of course, observe that we had a 'churchy' agenda. But would he feel that our meeting was in any other way different from a secular meeting of the Board of Directors or the Football Club Management Committee? Would he find a higher quality of listening, with fewer people trying to hold the floor, less exhibitionism, less merely destructive criticism, more careful attention being given to the views of others, less touchiness and readiness to take offence, more sensitivity, more mutual love? 'By this all men will know that you are my disciples, if you have love for one another.' Can we be sure that our debate will be stamped with this hallmark of discipleship? And if there is no observable difference of this kind, ought there to be? I believe the answer is overwhelmingly 'yes', and that this is one of the most seriously neglected of all the areas of our prayer.

1. LISTENING TO OURSELVES AND TO EACH OTHER

(a) When we discuss, and there is much at stake, it is natural that passions should run high. We are not alone in this. At the start of the first ever Council of the Christian Church, held in Jerusalem under the presidency of James, a younger brother of Jesus, we are told that there was fierce dissension and controversy. The issue was one of even more fundamental importance than is, say, the ordination of women in our own day. Christians of Jewish descent feared that if the tradition of full observance of the Mosaic Law was surrendered, the very foundations of the faith would have been cut away. It was agonizing for them. Yet such was the belief of all present that what was being looked for was not a human decision, but a discernment of the will of God, that 'the whole company fell silent and listened to Barnabas and Paul'. They were able to put fear and prejudice aside and really listen, and the message they heard was conclusive. God was able to speak to their hearts, and the decision that followed profoundly influenced the whole future development of the Church.

Do we sufficiently ponder this example? It is not always the same with us, is it? It is so easy to forget that Christ is not only the Goal but also the Way. Whenever we have a specific target ahead, our vision tends to narrow until we are aware only of that single objective. All our energies are concentrated on obtaining the 'right' decision, by which we invariably mean the decision that conforms with our own views. The good intentions about mutual tolerance and love which we had when we came to the meeting somehow vanish. Curiously, although we are always aware that others are not listening to us, we are hardly ever conscious that we are not listening to them. Our belief that somehow it is the other fellow who has the shortcomings goes very deep! There is a story about two eighteenth-century ministers who rode out together from Colchester to discuss spiritual matters. Finally, one said 'Well, brother, I can see that we shall not agree. You must continue to worship God in your way, and I will continue to worship him in his'!

So we need to have the humility to listen critically to ourselves, as well as the love that will enable us to listen to others. And there is no way to achieve this but by continuous prayer. When we invoke God's blessing on our meetings, we are at the same time offering ourselves to be changed in this way. Only thus can our work be continued and ended to the glory of God's holy name.

(b) But many people are wary of too much emphasis on tolerance in debate. They fear that 'understanding others' will degenerate into a bland cosiness in which no one dares to recognize sin and error for what they are. But God never requires us to buy peace at the price of truth. Sometimes it is right that anger should be voiced. It can have a cleansing quality that is much less harmful than the hidden pockets of venom in our relationships. But we cannot leave matters there. For Christians there is a compulsory second stage. Merely shouting people down and denouncing them achieves little or nothing. Usually its unadmitted purpose is to vindicate our own rightness. If we sincerely want to change other people's attitudes we have to attend to the anxieties and experiences that underlie what they say.

I saw a striking example of this while I was warden of a retreat house. One of the parish groups who visited the house had among their number a woman for whom nothing was ever right. Her continual criticism threatened to wreck the harmony of the whole weekend. In particular, when the time came for the Sunday Eucharist, she began to complain that 'you can't get a proper service these days'. The group decided that instead of arguing with her they would give her a special gift. They began, with enthusiasm, to arrange everything to suit her. She chose not only the form of service but the readings, the intercessions, the hymns, the flower arrangements and altar linen, and the good cause to which the offering should go. Half-way through the service her tears began to fall. It was the first time in her life that anyone had clearly shown her that she was worth their attention. I learned later that from that time her grumbling ceased, and she began to allow herself to be drawn into the fellowship of the group. Careful listening is a potent form of love.

2. LISTENING TO GOD

(a) But, you may say, meetings are too long as it is, and if we have to listen in this careful way, and spend more time in prayer, we shall be there all night. However, experience shows that the opposite is the case. For one result of a willingness to listen is that as individuals we talk less. And there is less need for recapitulation and revision, because people know that they have been properly heard in the first place. And, after a while, it begins to dawn on us that our differences may in themselves be part of God's plan for keeping us on course. If we were all radicals, change would come too fast and we would be at the mercy of untested ideas. If we were all traditionalists, change might not come at all and the work of the Holy Spirit would be impeded. God knows how many of each we need, to keep a true balance. So sharing our individual perceptions is an important part of our listening to God.

(b) But we can also listen to God in another more direct way which, mysteriously, seems to be independent of the opinions either of individuals or of the group. It is well described in the *Book of Discipline* of the Society of Friends:

> We do not seek a majority decision, or even consensus. We seek to discern the will of God. Listen, in the expectation that the right way will become clear. The way that opens may not be one that seemed obvious to anyone at the start of the meeting.

Quakers have no doubt whatsoever about the process through which God's intentions will be made clear. It is by means of continual pauses for silent reflection and prayer. Whenever differences seem irreconcilable and decisions hard to reach, the way forward may not lie in yet further argument. We need to wait upon God there and then, not afterwards on some other occasion. After such a pause it often happens that the resumed discussion takes a new and unforeseen direction. The Holy Spirit has had a chance to work in the silence. If our business meetings are not completely surrendered to God, they are a waste of time. Except the Lord build the house, they labour in vain that build it. Lord, we know that without you we are not able to please you. Grant that, in all our meetings, your Holy Spirit may direct and rule our hearts.

25

PRAYER IN THE COMMUNION OF SAINTS

Wherefore seeing we also are compassed about with so great a cloud of witnesses. . . .

HEBREWS 12.1 (AV)

From time to time on Sunday television we see religious programmes for which viewers are asked to select their favourite hymns. Always the same few appear in the 'top ten', and one of them is the evening hymn 'The day thou gavest'. Why is it so universally loved? Partly, perhaps, because it has one of those tunes which seem to gather up into themselves all the poignancy and joy of human life. But, above all, it is because of the inspiration of its theme, which at once lifts us out of the trivia and transience of our own little lives and makes us a part of something bigger, something infinitely glorious.

As o'er each continent and island
The dawn leads on another day
The voice of prayer is never silent
Nor dies the strain of praise away

When we sing this we do not need anyone to explain to us what is meant by 'the communion of saints'. And we instinctively know that we are encountering something even more awesome than the hymn suggests: the whole unseen company of heaven is joining in the praise. I do not know of any other thought which can give us greater support and encouragement in our daily discipline of prayer.

For, so often when we pray, we cannot help wondering what really is the point of our puny devotions and intercessions. What difference can my voice make in the immensity of the universe? But the truth is that it is never 'just me'. At any given hour of day or night, thousands of voices are reinforcing mine, and with them the voices of 'a vast throng, from every nation, of all tribes, peoples and languages, standing in front of the throne and before the Lamb'. Among these will be some whom we have known and loved, who are also joining in the chorus of praise. To be a part of this communion makes good our own insufficiencies, comforts us in loneliness, and gives us on earth a share in the joy of heaven. The pity is that so often we are unaware of this dimension of prayer.

1. COMMUNION IN LONELINESS

Of course the longing to be part of something bigger than oneself is basic to human nature. It accounts for so much of our behaviour, both good and bad, and we see it in every kind of group from Scouts to street gangs, and from football fans to political parties. In many groups membership has to be earned or paid for, in a variety of subtle ways. But to be part of the communion of saints is given to us as a free gift, available at all times and in all places. On Whitsunday, 1943, Dietrich Bonhoeffer wrote to his parents from prison:

> It is in quite a special way a feast of fellowship. I hardly felt lonely at all, for I was quite sure you were with me, and so were all the congregations with whom I have kept Whitsun in previous years.

And again, at Christmas:

> For a Christian there is nothing peculiarly difficult about Christmas in a prison cell. . . . Faith gives him a part in the communion of saints, a fellowship transcending the bounds of time and space and reducing the months of confinement here to insignificance.

We, too, in loneliness and pain can be given the sense of being with the company of Christ's beloved.

2. IN WEARINESS

Such an experience is available for us, too, at times when we feel devoid of all fire and spiritual energy. A verse in Psalm 134 speaks of those who 'stand by night in the house of the Lord', and Evelyn Underhill, a mystic of our own century, once wrote that at some time in our lives we are all 'called to serve on the night-shift'. Sometimes it may be that we do actually have to watch and wait through the night hours, or it may simply be that our soul is in darkness, but in either case the solace is the same. Perhaps as we try to pray at two o'clock in the morning we can picture in our imagination the countless others, in hospitals, in high-rise flats, in hotel bedrooms, who are our companions on the night shift. If I am awake in the night I sometimes think of a particular monastery chapel, a simple, tranquil place, and of the dark hills around it, and of the monks in the dimly lit stalls saying the night office. 'O Everlasting Jesus, who in the early hours of the morning didst give thyself to be reviled and scoffed at by thine enemies; visit us, we pray thee, at this hour with thy grace and mercy. . . .'

Many priests, too, would affirm the great help and sustenance they have received through faithfully carrying out what can seem an irksome duty—saying the daily office, often alone, often in an empty church. No one would underestimate the discipline required to turn out regularly, fresh or tired, in rain or snow, year in, year out. But they are sustained by the knowledge that many others are following the same rule, and so they build up a reserve of spiritual strength which is an unfailing resource. Perhaps lay people, too, could learn from this, and the possibility of making such a rule is something many of us could consider, in retirement, or when the children have grown up and left home.

3. IN AWARENESS OF THE ETERNAL

Strangely, the communion of saints is one of the aspects of spirituality which people outside the church can most easily feel. Once when I was visiting East Coker, as a pilgrim to the church where T. S. Eliot is buried, I found that the most recent signature in the visitors' book was that of another great poet, Philip Larkin, a life-long agnostic. He had stood in that quiet nave only hours before. I could be sure from what he wrote in his poem 'Church-going' that he had felt, as I did, the 'unignorable silence'. Despite his disbelief, he often felt a compulsion to visit churches, and to take off his hat and cycle-clips 'in awkward reverence'. Why is there this special indescribable atmosphere in our places of worship—including, of course, ruins? We would want to say that it is because of the presence of God. But God is equally present on the football ground and in the market place. The difference surely is that they are places where there has been a *response* to the presence of God, where prayer has been offered so long and so continually that it seems to have soaked into the very stones. The voices, the prayers, of all who have worshipped before us are enshrined there. And, of course, we still possess, and can use, prayers written by some of them; from the Saxon King, Alfred, to St Francis, Sir Thomas More, Ignatius Loyola, St John of the Cross, John Wesley, and many others. Most of us would have our own special lists, and to acquire such an anthology is an investment for life.

4. IN THE SUFFERING OF THE WORLD

Perhaps the area of prayer where, above all, we feel the wonder of this communion is in intercession. How inadequate we often feel if we are interceding alone. But for the whole church to be interceding—that is something different, a stupendous event in itself, a hallowing of the world's pain. Gonville ffrench-Beytagh writes of the cry that goes up from suffering millions:

> . . . a cry with no hope in it and no faith in it. But there is another cry, the cry of faith which arises from the church, and that cry needs to be as insistent and incessant as the cry of agony.

Wherever prayer is offered, by individuals, small groups, or scattered congregations, 'it has the intercessory function of becoming part of the cry of faith which mingles with the cry of agony and gives it the wings of faith'. In this way the many voices of the communion of saints lift up our individual voices to God.

5. IN DAILY LIFE

If all of this sounds beautiful and inspiring, well and good, for so it is. But as with all the other great truths of faith, there is another more earthy and ordinary aspect to it. In one of the famous letters written by C.S. Lewis, in which the experienced tempter, Screwtape, gives advice to his junior, Wormwood, there occurs the following passage:

> The great thing is to direct the patient's malice to his immediate neighbours whom he meets every day and to thrust his benevolence out to the remote circumstance, to people he does not know. The malice thus becomes wholly real and the benevolence largely imaginary.

To put it bluntly, it is no good luxuriating in beautiful thoughts of the communion of saints if we are rejecting our fellow pilgrims on earth. God does not play games! Only reality will do. 'If a man does not love his brother whom he has seen, how can he love God whom he has not seen?'—or love any of the saints, for that matter. Perhaps next time we are in church we might try taking with us an invisible supply of haloes and affixing one behind the head of each of our neighbours, since they are all called to be saints—St Shirley, St David, St Brian. Eventually we will come to ourselves. Is it possible that I too could belong to such a company, to such a communion? And the answer is, of course, that through the incomprehensible mercy of God, I already do.